*THE HOME UNIVERSITY LIBRARY*
*OF MODERN KNOWLEDGE*

121

# POLITICAL THOUGHT
# IN ENGLAND

## LOCKE *to* BENTHAM

# POLITICAL THOUGHT IN ENGLAND

## IN ENGLAND

*Locke to Bentham*

HAROLD J. *Joseph* LASKI

LONDON

**OXFORD UNIVERSITY PRESS**

NEW YORK   TORONTO

*First published in* 1920 *and reprinted in* 1922, 1925,
1927, 1930, 1932, *and* 1937. *Reset in* 1949
*and reprinted in* 1950, 1955 *and* 1961

**PRINTED IN GREAT BRITAIN**

## NOTE

It is impossible for me to publish this book without some expression of the debt it owes to Leslie Stephen's *History of the English Thought in the Eighteenth Century*. It is almost insolent to praise such work; but I may be permitted to say that no one can fully appreciate either its wisdom or its knowledge who has not had to dig among the original texts.

Were so small a volume worthy to bear a dedication, I should associate it with the name of my friend Walter Lippmann. He and I have so often discussed the substance of its problems that I am certain a good deal of what I feel to be my own is, where it has merit, really his. This volume is thus in great part a tribute to him; though there is little that can repay such friendship as he gives.

H. J. L.

HARVARD UNIVERSITY
15 *September* 1919

# CONTENTS

# CHAPTER I

# INTRODUCTION

THE eighteenth century may be said to begin with the
Revolution of 1688; for, with its completion, the dogma
of Divine Right disappeared for ever from English
politics. Its place was but partially filled until Hume
and Burke supplied the outlines of a new philosophy.
For the observer of this age can hardly fail, as he notes
its relative barrenness of abstract ideas, to be impressed
by the large part Divine Right must have played in the
politics of the succeeding century. Its very absoluteness
made for keen partisanship on the one side and the
other. It could produce at once the long-winded rhap-
sodies of Filmer and, by repulsion, the wearisome
reiterations of Algernon Sidney. Once the foundations
of Divine Right had been destroyed by Locke, the basis
of passionate controversy was absent. The theory of a
social contract never produced in England the enthusiasm it evoked in France, for the simple reason that
the main objective of Rousseau and his disciples had
already been secured there by other weapons. And this
has perhaps given to the eighteenth century an urbane-
ness from which its predecessor was largely free. Sermons
are perhaps the best test of such a change; and it is a relief to move from the addresses bristling with Suarez and
Bellarmine to the noble exhortations of Bishop Butler.
Not until the French Revolution were ultimate dogmas
again called into question; and it is about them only that
political speculation provokes deep feeling. The urbanity,

9

indeed, is not entirely new. The Restoration had heralded
its coming, and the tone of Halifax has more in common
with Bolingbroke and Hume than with Hobbes and
Filmer. Nor has the eighteenth century an historical
profundity to compare with that of the zealous pamphleteers in the seventeenth. Heroic archivists like
Prynne find very different substitutes in brilliant
journalists like Defoe, and if Dalrymple and Blackstone
are respectable, they bear no comparison with masters
like Selden and Sir Henry Spelman.

Yet urbanity must not deceive us. The eighteenth
century has an importance in English politics which the
comparative absence of systematic speculation cannot
conceal. If its large constitutional outlines had been
traced by a preceding age, its administrative detail had
still to be secured. The process was very gradual; and the
attempt of George III to arrest it produced the splendid
effort of Edmund Burke. Locke's work may have been
not seldom confused and stumbling; but it gave to the
principle of consent a permanent place in English politics.
It is the age which saw the crystallization of the party-
system, and therein it may perhaps lay claim to have
recognized what Bagehot called the vital principle of
representative government. Few discussions of the sphere
of government have been so productive as that in which
Adam Smith gave a new basis to economic science.
Few controversies have, despite its dullness, so carefully
investigated the eternal problem of Church and State as
that to which Hoadly's bishopric contributed its name.
De Lolme is the real parent of that interpretative analysis
which has, in Bagehot's hands, become not the least
fruitful type of political method. Blackstone, in a real
sense, may be called the ancestor of Professor Dicey.

The very calmness of the atmosphere only the more surely paved the way for the surprising novelties of Godwin and the revolutionists.

Nor must we neglect the relation between its ethics and its politics. The eighteenth-century school of British moralists has suffered somewhat beside the greater glories of Berkeley and Hume. Yet it was a great work to which they bent their effort, and they knew its greatness. The deistic controversy involved a fresh investigation of the basis of morals; and it is to the credit of the investigators that they attempted to provide it in social terms. It is, indeed, one of the primary characteristics of the British mind to be interested in problems of conduct rather than of thought. The seventeenth century had, for the most part, been interested in theology, and government; and its preoccupation, in both domains, with supernatural sanctions, made its conclusions unfitted for a period dominated by rationalism. Locke regarded his *Human Understanding* as the preliminary to an ethical inquiry; and Hume seems to have considered his *Principles of Morals* the most vital of his works. It may be true, as the mordant insight of Mark Pattison suggested, that 'those periods in which morals have been represented as the proper study of man, and his only business, have been periods of spiritual abasement and poverty'. Certainly no one will be inclined to claim for the eighteenth century the spiritual idealism of the seventeenth, though Law and Bishop Wilson and the Wesleyan revival will make us generalize with caution. But the truth was that theological ethics had become empty and inadequate, and the problem was therefore urgent. That is why Shaftesbury, Hutcheson, Hume, and Adam Smith—to take only men of the first eminence—

were thinking not less for politics than for ethics when they sought to justify the ways of man to man. For all of them saw that a theory of society is impossible without the provision of psychological foundations; and those must, above all, result in a theory of conduct if the social bond is to be maintained. That sure insight is, of course, one current only in a greater English stream which reaches back to Hobbes at its source and forward to T. H. Green at perhaps its fullest. Its value is its denial of politics as a science distinct from other human relations; and that is why Adam Smith can write of moral sentiments no less than of the wealth of nations. The eighteenth century saw clearly that each aspect of social life must find its place in the political equation.

Yet it is undoubtedly an age of methods rather than of principles; and, as such, its peaceful prosperity was well suited to its questions. Problems of technique, such as the Cabinet and the Bank of England, required the absence of passionate debate if they were in any fruitful fashion to be solved. Nor must the achievement of the age in politics be minimized. It was, of course, a complacent time; but we ought to note that foreigners of distinction did not wonder at its complacency. Voltaire and Montesquieu look back to England in the eighteenth century for the substance of political truths. The American colonies took alike their methods and their arguments from English ancestors; and Burke provided them with the main elements of justification. The very quietness, indeed, of the time was the natural outcome of a century of storm; and England surely had some right to be contented when her political system was compared with the governments of France and Germany. Not, indeed, that the full fruit of the Revolution was gathered. The principle of consent came, in practice and till 1760, to mean the government of the Whig Oligarchy; and the *Extraordinary Black Book* remains to tell us what happened when George III gave the Tory party a new lease of power. There is throughout the time an over-emphasis upon the value of order, and a not unnatural tendency to confound the private good of the governing class with the general welfare of the State. It became the fixed policy of Walpole to make prosperity the mask for political stagnation. He turned political debate from principles to personalities, and a sterile generation was the outcome of his cunning.

Not that this barrenness is without its compensations. The theories of the Revolution had exhausted their fruitfulness within a generation. The constitutional ideas of the seventeenth century had no substance for an England where Anglicanism and agriculture were beginning to lose the rigid outlines of overwhelming predominance. What was needed was the assurance of safety for the Church that her virtue might be tested in the light of noncomformist practice on the one hand, and the new rationalism on the other. What was needed also was the expansion of English commerce into the new channels opened for it by the victories of Chatham. Mr. Chief Justice Holt had given it the legal categories it would require; and Hume and Adam Smith were to explain that commerce might grow with small danger to agricultural prosperity. Beneath the apparent calm of Walpole's rule new forces were fast stirring. That can be seen on every side. The sturdy morality of Johnson, the new literary forms of Richardson and Fielding, the theatre which Garrick founded upon the ruins produced by Collier's indignation, the revival of which Law and

Wesley are the great symbols, show that the stagnation was sleep rather than death. The needed events of shock were close at hand. The people of England would never have discovered the real meaning of 1688 if George III had not denied its principles. When he enforced the resignation of the elder Pitt the theories at once of Edmund Burke and English radicalism were born; for the *Present Discontents* and the *Society for the Support of the Bill of Rights* are the dawn of a splendid recovery. And they made possible the speculative ferment which showed that England was at last awake to the meaning of Montesquieu and Rousseau. Just as the shock of the Lancastrian wars produced the Tudor despotism, so did the turmoil of civil strife produce the complacency of the eighteenth century. But the peace of the Tudors was the death-bed of the Stuarts; and it was the stagnant optimism of the early eighteenth century which made possible the birth of democratic England.

The atmosphere of the time, in fact, is deep-rooted in the conditions of the past. Locke could not have written had not Hobbes and Filmer defended in set terms the ideal of despotic government. He announced the advent of the modern system of parliamentary government; and from his time the debate has been rather of the conditions under which it is to work, than of the foundations upon which it is based. Burke, for example, wrote what constitutes the supreme analysis of the statesman's art. Adam Smith discussed in what fashion the prosperity of peoples could be best advanced. From Locke, that is to say, the subject of discussion is rather *politik* than *staatslehre*. The great debate inaugurated by the Reformation ceased when Locke had outlined an intelligible basis for parliamentary government. Hume, Bolingbroke,

Burke, are all of them concerned with the detail of political arrangement in a fashion which presupposes the acceptance of basis previously known. Burke, indeed, toward the latter part of his life, awoke to the realization that men were dissatisfied with the traditional substance of the State. But he met the new desires with hate instead of understanding, and the Napoleonic wars drove the current of democratic opinion underground. Hall and Owen and Hodgskin inherited the thoughts of Ogilvie and Spence and Paine; and if they did not give them substance, at least they gave them form for a later time.

Nor is the reason for this preoccupation far to seek. The advance of English politics in the preceding two centuries was mainly an advance of structure; yet relative at least to continental fact, it appeared liberal enough to hide the disharmonies of its inner content. The King was still a mighty influence. The power of the aristocracy was hardly broken until the Reform Bill of 1867. The Church continued to dominate the political aspect of English religious life until, after 1832, new elements alien from her ideals were introduced into the House of Commons. The conditions of change lay implicit in the Industrial Revolution, when a new class of men attained control of the nation's economic power. Only then was a realignment of political forces essential. Only then, that is to say, had the time arrived for a new theory of the State.

The political ideas of the eighteenth century are thus in some sort a comment upon the system established by the Revolution; and this is, in its turn, the product of the struggle between Parliament and Crown in the preceding age. But we cannot understand the eighteenth century, or its theories, unless we realize that its temper was still dominantly aristocratic. From no accusation were its statesmen more anxious to be free than from that of a belief in democratic government. Whether Whigs or Tories were in power, it was always the great families who ruled. For them the Church, at least in its higher branches, existed; and the difference between nobleman and commoner at Oxford is as striking as it is hideous to this generation. For them also literature and the theatre made their display; and if Dr. Johnson could heap an immortal contumely upon the name of patron, we all know of the reverence he felt in the presence of the king. Divine Right and non-resistance were dead, but they had not died without a struggle. Freedom of the press and legal equality may have been obtained; but it was not until the passage of Fox's Libel Act that the first became secure, and J. L. and Barbara Hammond have recently illumined for us the inward meaning of the second. The populace might, on occasion, be strong enough to force the elder Pitt upon an unwilling king, or to shout for Wilkes and liberty against the unconstitutional usurpation of the monarch-ridden House of Commons. Such outbursts are yet the exception to the prevailing temper. The deliberations of Parliament were still, at least technically, a secret; and membership therein, save for one or two anomalies like Westminster and Bristol, was still the private possession of a privileged class. The Revolution, in fact, meant less an abstract and general freedom, than a special release from the arbitrary will of a stupid monarch who aroused against himself every deep-seated prejudice of his generation. The England which sent James II upon his travels may be, as Hume pointed out, reduced to a pathetic fragment

even of its electorate. The masses were unknown and
undiscovered, or, where they emerged, it was either to
protest against some wise reform like Walpole's Excise
Scheme, or to become, as in Goldsmith and Cowper and
Crabbe, the object of half-pitying poetic sentiment. How
deep-rooted was the notion of aristocratic control was
to be shown when France turned into substantial fact
Rousseau's demand for freedom. The protest of Burke
against its supposed anarchy swept England like a
flame; and only a courageous handful could be found
to protest against Pitt's prostitution of her freedom.

Such an age could make but little pretence to discovery; and, indeed, it is most largely absent from its
speculation. In its political ideas this is necessarily and
especially the case. For the State is at no time an un-
changing organization; it reflects with singular exactness
the dominating ideas of its environment. That division
into government and subjects which is its main characteristic is here noteworthy for the narrowness of the class
from which the government is derived, and the consistent inertia of those over whom it rules. There is
curiously little controversy over the seat of sovereign
power. That is with most men acknowledged to reside
in the king in Parliament. What balance of forces is
necessary to its most perfect equilibrium may arouse
dissension when George III forgets the result of half a
century's evolution. Junius may have to explain in in-
vective what Burke magistrally demonstrated in terms
of political philosophy. But the deeper problems of the
State lay hidden until Bentham and the revolutionists
came to insist upon their presence. That did not mean
that the eighteenth century was a soulless failure. Rather
did it mean that a period of transition had been success-

B

fully bridged. The stage was set for a new effort simply because the theories of the older philosophy no longer represented the facts at issue.

It was thus Locke only in this period who confronted the general problems of the modern State. Other thinkers assumed his structure and dealt with the details he left undetermined. The main problems, the Church apart, arose when a foreigner occupied the English throne and left the methods of government to those who were acquainted with them. That most happy of all the happy accidents in English history made Walpole the fundamental statesman of the time. He used his opportunity to the full. Inheriting the possibilities of the Cabinet system he gave it its modern expression by creating the office of Prime Minister. The party-system was already inevitable; and with his advent to full power in 1727 we have the characteristic outlines of English representative government. Thenceforward, there are, on the whole, but three large questions with which the age concerned itself. Toleration had already been won by the persistent necessities of two generations, and the noble determination of William III; but the place of the Church in the Revolution State and the nature of that State were still undetermined. Hoadly had one solution, Law another; and the genial rationalism of the time, coupled with the political affiliations of the High Church party, combined to give Hoadly the victory; but his opponents, and Law especially, remained to be the parents of a movement for ecclesiastical freedom of which it has been the good fortune of Oxford to supply in each succeeding century the leaders. America presented again the problem of consent in the special perspective of the imperial relation; and the decision which grew out of the blundering obscurantism of the king enabled Burke nobly to restate and amply to revivify the principles of 1688. Chatham meanwhile had stumbled upon a vaster empire; and the industrial system which his effort quickened could not live under an economic régime which still bore traces of the narrow nationalism of the Tudors. No man was so emphatically representative of his epoch as Adam Smith; and no thinker has ever stated in such generous terms the answer of his time to the most vital of its questions. The answer, indeed, like all good answers, revealed rather the difficulty of the problem than the prospect of its solution; though nothing so clearly heralded the new age that was coming than his repudiation of the past in terms of a real appreciation of it. The American War and the two great revolutions brought a new race of thinkers into being. The French seed at last produced its harvest. Bentham absorbed the purpose of Rousseau even while he rejected his methods. For a time, indeed, the heat and dust of war obscured the issue that Bentham raised. But the certainties of the future lay on his side.

## CHAPTER II

# THE PRINCIPLES OF THE REVOLUTION

## I

THE English Revolution was in the main a protest against the attempt of James II to establish a despotism in alliance with France and Rome. It was almost entirely a movement of the aristocracy, and, for the most part, it was aristocratic opposition that it encountered. What it did was to make for ever impossible the thought of reunion with Rome and the theory that the throne could be established on any other basis than the consent of Parliament. For no one could pretend that William of Orange ruled by Divine Right. The scrupulous shrank from proclaiming the deposition of James; and the fiction that he had abdicated was not calculated to deceive the warmest of William's adherents. An unconstitutional Parliament thereupon declared the throne vacant; and after much negotiation William and Mary were invited to occupy it. To William the invitation was irresistible. It gave him the assistance of the first maritime power in Europe against the imperialism of Louis XIV. It ensured the survival of Protestantism against the encroachment of an enemy who never slumbered. Nor did England find the new régime unwelcome. Every widespread conviction of her people had been wantonly outraged by the blundering stupidity of James. If a large fraction of the English Church held aloof from the new order on technical grounds, the commercial classes gave it their warm support; and many who doubted in theory submitted in practice. All at least were conscious that a new era had dawned.

For William had come over with a definite purpose in view. James had wrought havoc with what the Civil Wars had made the essence of the English constitution; and it had become important to define in set terms the conditions upon which the life of kings must in the future be regulated. The reign of William is nothing so much as the period of that definition; and the fortunate discovery was made of the mechanisms whereby its translation into practice might be secured. The Bill of Rights (1689) and the Act of Settlement (1701) are the foundation stones of the modern constitutional system.

What, broadly, was established was the dependence of the Crown upon Parliament. Finance and the army were brought under Parliamentary control by the simple expedient of making its annual summons essential. The right of petition was re-affirmed; and the independence of the judges and ministerial responsibility were secured by the same Act which forever excluded the legitimate heirs from their royal inheritance. It is difficult not to be amazed at the almost casual fashion in which so striking a revolution was effected. Not, indeed, that the solution worked easily at the outset. William remained to the end a foreigner, who could not understand the inwardness of English politics. It was the necessities of foreign policy which drove him to admit the immense possibilities of the party-system as also to accept his own best safeguard in the foundation of the Bank of England. The Cabinet, towards the close of his reign, had already become the fundamental administrative instrument. Originally a committee of the Privy Council, it had no party basis until the ingenious Sunderland atoned for a score of dishonesties by insisting that the root of its efficiency would be found in its selection from a single party. William acquiesced but doubtfully; for, until the end of his life, he never understood why his ministers should not be a group of able counsellors chosen without reference to their political affiliations. Sunderland knew better for the simple reason that he belonged to that period when the Whigs and Tories had gambled against each other for their heads. He knew that no council-board could with comfort contain both himself and Halifax; just as William himself was to learn quite early that neither honour nor confidence could win un-swerving support from John Churchill. There is a certain feverishness in the atmosphere of the reign which shows how many kept an anxious eye on St. Germain even while they attended the morning levee at Whitehall.

What secured the permanence of the settlement was less the policy of William than the blunder of the French monarch. Patience, foresight, and generosity had not availed to win for William more than a grudging recog-nition of his kingship. He had received only a half-hearted support for his foreign policy. The army, de-spite his protests, had been reduced; and the enforced return of his own Dutch Guards to Holland was de-liberately conceived to cause him pain. But at the very moment when his strength seemed weakest James II died; and Louis XIV, despite written obligation, sought to comfort the last moments of his tragic exile by the falsely chivalrous recognition of the Old Pretender as the rightful English king. It was a terrible mistake. It did for William what no action of his own could ever have achieved. It suggested that England must receive its ruler at the hands of a foreign sovereign. The national pride of the people rallied to the cause for which William stood. He was king—so, at least in contrast to Louis's decision, it appeared—by their deliberate choice and the settlement of which he was the symbol would be maintained. Parliament granted to William all that his foreign policy could have demanded. His own death was only the prelude to the victories of Marlborough. Those victories seemed to seal the solution of 1688. A moment came when sentiment and intrigue combined to throw in jeopardy the Act of Settlement. But Death held the stakes against the gambler's throw of Bolingbroke; and the accession of George I assured the permanence of Revolution principles.

## II

The theorist of the Revolution is Locke; and it was his conscious effort to justify the innovations of 1688. He sought, as he said, ' to establish the throne of our great Restorer, our present King William, and make good his title in the consent of the people '. In the debate which followed, his argument remained unanswered, for the sufficient reason that it had the common sense of the generation on its side. Yet Locke has suffered not a little at the hands of succeeding thinkers. Though his influence upon his own time was immense; though Montesquieu owed to him the acutest of his insights; though the principles of the American Revolution are in large part an acknowledged adoption of his own; he has become one of the political classics who are taken for granted rather than read. It is a profound and regrettable error. Locke may not possess the clarity and ruthless logic of Hobbes, nor the genius for compressing into a phrase the experience of a lifetime which makes Burke the first of English political thinkers. He yet stated more clearly than either the general problem of the modern State. Hobbes, after all, worked with an impossible psychology and sought no more than the prescription against disorder. Burke wrote rather a textbook for the cautious administrator than a guide for the liberal statesman. But Locke saw that the main problem of the State is the conquest of freedom and it was for its definition in terms of individual good that he above all strove.

Much, doubtless, of his neglect is due to the medium in which he worked. He wrote at a time when the social contract seemed the only possible retort to the theory of Divine Right. He so emphasized the principle of consent that when contractualism came in its turn to be discarded, it was discovered that Locke suffered far more than Hobbes by the change so made. For Hobbes cared nothing for the contract so long as strong government could be shown to be implicit in the natural badness of men, while Locke assumed their goodness and made his contract essential to their opportunity for moral expression. Nor did he, like Rousseau, seize upon the organic nature of the State. To him the State was always a mere aggregate, and the convenient simplicity of majority-rule solved, for him, the vital political problems. But Rousseau was translated into the complex dialectic of Hegel and lived to become the parent of theories he would have doubtless been the first to disown. Nor was Locke aided by his philosophic outlook. Few great thinkers have so little perceived the psychological foundations of politics. What he did was rather to fasten upon the great institutional necessity of his time—the provision of channels of assent—and emphasize its importance to the seclusion of all other factors. The problem is in fact more complex; and the solution he indicated became so natural a part of the political fabric that the value of his emphasis upon its import was largely forgotten when men again took up the study of foundations.

John Locke was born at Wrington in Somerset on the 29th of August, 1632. His father was clerk to the county justices and acted as a captain in a cavalry regiment during the Civil War. Though he suffered heavy losses, he was able to give his son as good an education as the time afforded. Westminster under Dr. Busby may not have been the gentlest of academies, but at least it provided Locke with an admirable training in the classics. He himself, indeed, in the *Thoughts on Education* doubted the value of such exercises; nor does he seem to have conceived any affection for Oxford whither he proceeded in 1652 as a junior student of Christ Church. The university was then under the Puritan control of Dr. John Owen; but not even his effort to redeem the university from its reputation for intellectual laxity rescued it from the ' wrangling and ostentation ' of the peripatetic philosophy. Yet it was at Oxford that he encountered the work of Descartes which first attracted him to metaphysics. There, too, he met Pocock, the Arabic scholar, and Wallis, the mathematician, who must at least have commanded his respect. In 1659 he accepted a Senior Studentship of his college, which he retained until he was deemed politically undesirable in 1684. After toying with his father's desire that he should enter the Church, he began the study of medicine. Scientific interest won for him the friendship of Boyle; and while he was administering physic to the patients of Dr. Thomas, he was making the observations recorded in Boyle's *History of the Air* which Locke himself edited after the death of his friend.

Meanwhile accident had turned his life into far different paths. An appointment as secretary to a special ambassador opened up to him a diplomatic career; but his sturdy common sense showed him his unfitness for such labours. After his visit to Prussia he returned to Oxford, and there, in 1667, in the course of his medical work, he met Anthony Ashley, the later Lord Shaftesbury and the Achitophel of Dryden's great satire. The two men were warmly attracted to each other, and Locke accepted an appointment as physician to Lord Ashley's household. But he was also much more than this. The tutor of Ashley's philosophic grandson, he became also his patron's confidential counsellor. In 1663 he became part author of a constitutional scheme for Carolina which is noteworthy for its emphasis, thus early, upon the importance of religious toleration. In 1672, when Ashley became Lord Chancellor, he became Secretary of Presentations and, until 1675, Secretary to the Council of Trade and Foreign Plantations. Meanwhile he carried on his medical work and must have obtained some reputation in it; for he is honourably mentioned by Sydenham, in his *Method of Curing Fevers* (1676), and had been elected to the Royal Society in 1668. But his real genius lay in other directions.

Locke himself has told us how a few friends began to meet at his chamber for the discussions of questions which soon passed into metaphysical inquiry; and a page from a commonplace book of 1671 is the first beginning of his systematic work. Relieved of his administrative duties in 1675, he spent the next four years in France, mainly occupied with medical observation. He returned to England in 1679 to assist Lord Shaftesbury in the passionate debates upon the Exclusion Bill. Locke followed his patron into exile, remaining abroad from 1683 until the Revolution. Deprived of his fellowship in 1684 through the malice of Charles II, he would have been without means of support had not Shaftesbury bequeathed him a pension. As it was, he had no easy time. His extradition was demanded by James II after the Monmouth rebellion; and though he was later pardoned he refused to return to England until William of Orange had procured his freedom. A year after his return he made his appearance as a writer. The *Essay Concerning Human Understanding* and the *Two Treatises of Government* were both published in 1690. Five years earlier the *Letter Concerning Toleration* was published in its Latin dress; and four years afterwards an English translation appeared. This last, however, perhaps on grounds of expediency, Locke never acknowledged until his will was published; for the time was not yet suited to such generous speculations. Locke was thus in his fifty-eighth year when his first admitted work appeared. But the rough attempts at the *Essay* date from 1671, and hints towards the *Letter on Toleration* can be found in fragments of various dates between the twenty-eighth and thirty-fifth years of his life. Of the *Two Treatises* the first seems to have been written between 1680 and 1685, the second in the last year of his Dutch exile.[1]

The remaining fourteen years of Locke's life were

[1] On the evidence for these dates see the convincing argument of H. R. Fox-Bourne in his *Life of Locke*, Vol. II, pp. 165-7.

passed in semi-retirement in East Anglia. Though he held public office, first as Commissioner of Appeals, and later of Trade, for twelve years, he could not stand the pressure of London winters, and his public work was only intermittent. His counsel, nevertheless, was highly valued; and he seems to have won no small confidence from William in diplomatic matters. Somers and Charles Montagu held him in high respect, and he had the warm friendship of Sir Isaac Newton. He published some short discussions on economic matters, and in 1695 gave valuable assistance in the destruction of the censorship of the press. Two years earlier he had published his *Thoughts on Education*, in which the observant reader may find the germ of most of Emile's ideas. He did not fail to revise the *Essay* from time to time; and his *Reasonableness of Christianity*, which, through Toland, provoked a reply from Stillingfleet and showed Locke in retort a master of the controversial art, was in some sort the foundation of the deistic debate in the next epoch. But his chief work had already been done, and he spent his energies in rewarding the affection of his friends. Locke died on 28 October 1704, amid circumstances of singular majesty. He had lived a full life, and few have so completely realized the medieval ideal of specializing in omniscience. He left warm friends behind him; and Lady Masham has said of him that beyond which no man may dare to aspire.[1]

[1] Fox-Bourne, *op. cit.* Letter from Lady Masham to Jean le Clerc.

## III

Locke's *Two Treatises of Government* are different both in object and in value. The first is a detailed and tiresome response to the historic imagination of Sir Robert Filmer. In his *Patriarcha*, which first saw the light in 1680, though it had been written long before, the latter had sought to reach the ultimate conclusion of Hobbes without the element of contract upon which the great thinker depended. ' I consent with him ', said Filmer of Hobbes, ' about the Rights of *exercising* Government, but I cannot agree to his means of acquiring it.' That power must be absolute, Filmer, like Hobbes, has no manner of doubt; but his method of proof is to derive the title of Charles I from Adam. Little difficulties like the origin of primogeniture, or whence, as Locke points out, the universal monarchy of Shem can be derived, the good Sir Robert does not satisfactorily determine. Locke takes him up point by point, and there is little enough left, save a sense that history is the root of institutions, when he has done. What troubles us is rather why Locke should have wasted the resources of his intelligence upon so feeble an opponent. The book of Hobbes lay ready to his hand; yet he almost ostentatiously refused to grapple with it. The answer doubtless lies in Hobbes's unsavoury fame. The man who made the Church a mere department of the State and justified not less the title of Cromwell than of the Stuarts was not the opponent for one who had a very practical problem in hand. And Locke could answer that he was answering Hobbes implicitly in the second *Treatise*. And though Filmer might never have been known had not Locke thus honoured him by retort, he doubtless symbolized what many a nobleman's chaplain preached to his master's dependants at family prayers.

The second *Treatise* goes to the root of the matter. Why does political power, ' a Right of making Laws and Penalties of Death and consequently all less Penalties ', exist? It can only be for the public benefit, and our inquiry is thus a study of the grounds of political obedience. Locke thus traverses the ground Hobbes had covered in his *Leviathan* though he rejects every premise of the earlier thinker. To Hobbes the state of nature which precedes political organization had been a state of war. Neither peace nor reason could prevail where every man was his neighbour's enemy; and the establishment of absolute power, with the consequent surrender by men of all their natural liberties, was the only means of escape from so brutal a régime. That the state of nature was so distinguished Locke at the outset denies. The state of nature is governed by the law of nature. The law of nature is not, as Hobbes had made it, the antithesis of real law, but rather its condition antecedent. It is a body of rules which governs, at all times and all places, the conduct of men. Its arbiter is reason and, in the natural state, reason shows us that men are equal. From this equality are born men's natural rights which Locke, like the Independents in the Puritan Revolution, identifies with life, liberty, and property. Obviously enough, as Hobbes had also granted, the instinct to self-preservation is the deepest of human impulses. By liberty Locke means the right of the individual to follow his own bent granted only his observance of the law of nature. Law, in such an aspect, is clearly a means to the realization of freedom in the same way that the rule of the road will, by its common acceptance, save its observers from accident. It promotes the initiative of men by defining in terms which by their very statement obtain acknowledgement the conditions upon which individual caprice may have its play. Property Locke derives from a primitive communism which becomes transmuted into individual ownership whenever a man has mingled his labour with some object. This labour theory of ownership lived, it may be remarked, to become, in the hands of Hodgskin and Thompson, the parent of modern socialism.

The state of nature is thus in contrast to the argument of Hobbes, pre-eminently social in character. There may be war or violence; but that is only when men have abandoned the rule of reason which is integral to their character. But the state of nature is not a civil State. There is no common superior to enforce the law of nature. Each man, as best he may, works out his own interpretation of it. But because the intelligences of men are different there is an inconvenient variety in the conceptions of justice. The result is uncertainty and chaos; and means of escape must be found from a condition which the weakness of men must ultimately make intolerable. It is here that the social contract emerges. But just as Locke's natural state implies a natural man utterly distinct from Hobbes's gloomy picture, so does Locke's social contract represent rather the triumph of reason than of hard necessity. It is a contract of each with all, a surrender by the individual of his personal right to fulfil the commands of the law of nature in return for the guarantee that his rights as nature ordains them—life and liberty and property—will be preserved. The contract is thus not general as with Hobbes but

limited and specific in character. Nor is it, as Hobbes
made it, the resignation of power into the hands of some
single man or group. On the contrary, it is a contract
with the community as a whole which thus becomes
that common political superior—the State—which is to
enforce the law of nature and punish infractions of it.
Nor is Locke's state a sovereign State: the very word
'sovereignty' does not occur, significantly enough,
throughout the treatise. The State has power only for
the protection of natural law. Its province ends when
it passes beyond those boundaries.

Such a contract, in Locke's view, involves the pre-
eminent necessity of majority-rule. Unless the minority
is content to be bound by the will of superior numbers
the law of nature has no more protection than it had
before the institution of political society. And it is further
to be assumed that the individual has surrendered to the
community his individual right of carrying out the judgement involved in natural law. Whether Locke conceived the contract so formulated to be historical, it is
no easy matter to determine. That no evidence of its
early existence can be adduced he ascribes to its origin
in the infancy of the race; and the histories of Rome
and Sparta and Venice seem to him proof that the
theory is somehow demonstrable by facts. More important than origins, he seems to deem its implications.
He has placed consent in the foreground of the argument; and he was anxious to establish the grounds for
its continuance. Can the makers of the original contract,
that is to say, bind their successors? If legitimate government is based upon the consent of its subjects, may
they withdraw their consent? And what of a child born
into the community? Locke is at least logical in his

consent. The contract of obedience must be free or else, as Hooker had previously insisted, it is not a contract. Yet Locke urged that the primitive members of a State are bound to its perpetuation simply because unless the majority had power to enforce obedience, government, in any satisfactory sense, would be impossible. With children the case is different. They are born subjects of no government or country; and their consent to its laws must either be derived from express acknowledge-ment, or by the tacit implication of the fact that the protection of the State has been accepted. But no one is bound until he has shown by the rule of his mature conduct that he considers himself a common subject with his fellows. Consent implies an act of will and we must have evidence to infer its presence before the rule of subjection can be applied.

We have thus the State, though the method of its organization is not yet outlined. For Locke there is a difference, though he did not explicitly describe its nature, between State and Government. Indeed he sometimes approximates, without formally adopting, the attitude of Pufendorf, his great German contemporary, where government is derived from a secondary contract dependent upon the original institution of civil society. The distinction is made in the light of what is to follow. For Locke was above all anxious to leave supreme power in a community whose single will, as manifested by majority-verdict, could not be challenged by any lesser organ than itself. Government there must be if political society is to endure; but its form and substance are dependent upon popular institution.

Locke follows in the great Aristotelian tradition of dividing the types of government into three. Where the

c

power of making laws is in a single hand we have a
monarchy; where it is exercised by a few or all we have
alternatively oligarchy and democracy. The disposition
of the legislative power is the fundamental test of type;
for executive and judiciary are clearly dependent on
it. Nor, as Hobbes argued, is the form of government
permanent in character; the supreme community is as
capable of making temporary as of registering irrevocable
decisions. And though Locke admits that monarchy,
from its likeness to the family, is the most primitive type
of government, he denies Hobbes's assertion that it is
the best. It seems, in his view, always to degenerate
into the hands of lesser men who betray the contract
they were appointed to observe. Nor is oligarchy much
better off since it emphasizes the interest of a group
against the superior interest of the community as a
whole. Democracy alone proffers adequate safeguards of
an enduring good rule; a democracy, that is to say,
which is in the hands of delegates controlled by popular
election. Not that Locke is anxious for the abolition of
kingship. His letters show that he disliked the Cromwellian system and the republicanism which Harrington
and Milton had based upon it. He was content to have
a kingship divested of legislative power so long as hereditary succession was acknowledged to be dependent
upon popular consent. The main thing was to be rid
of the Divine Right of kings.

We have thus an organ for the interpretation of
natural law free from shifting variety of individual judgement. We have a means for securing impartial justice
between members of civil society, and to that means the
force of men has been surrendered. The formulation of
the rules by which life, liberty, and property are to be

secured is legislation and this, from the terms of the
original contract, is the supreme function of the State.
But, in Locke's view, two other functions still remain.
Law has not only to be declared. It must be enforced;
and the business of the executive is to secure obedience
to the command of law. But Locke here makes a third
distinction. The State must live with other States, both
as regards its individual members, and as a collective
body; and the power which deals with this aspect of its
relationships, Locke termed 'federative'. This last distinction, indeed, has no special value; and its author's
own defence of it is far from clear. More important,
especially for future history, was his emphasis on the
distinction between legislature and executive. The
making of laws is for Locke a relatively simple and
rapid task; the legislature may do its work and be gone.
But those who attend to their execution must be ceaseless in their vigilance. It is better, therefore, to separate
the two both as to powers and persons. Otherwise
legislators 'may exempt themselves from obedience to
the laws they make, and suit the law, both in its making
and its execution, to their own private wish, and thereby
come to have a distinct interest from the rest of the
community, contrary to the end of society and government'. The legislator must therefore be bound by his
own laws; and he must be chosen in such fashion that
the representative assembly may fairly represent its con-
stituencies. It was the patent anomalies of the existent
scheme of distribution which made Locke here proffer
his famous suggestion that the rotten boroughs should
be abolished by executive act. One hundred and forty
years were still to pass before this wise suggestion was
translated into statute.

Though Locke thus insisted upon the separation of powers, he realized that emergencies are the parent of special need; and he recognized that not only may the executive, as in England, share in the task of legislation, but also may issue ordinances when the legislature is not in session, or act contrary to law in case of grave danger. Nor can the executive be forced to summon the legislature. Here, clearly enough, Locke is generalizing from the English constitution; and its sense of compromise is implicit in his remarks. Nor is his surrender here of consent sufficient to be inconsistent with his general outlook. For at the back of each governmental act, there is, in his own mind, an active citizen body occupied in judging it with single-minded reference to the law of nature and their own natural rights. There is thus a standard of right and wrong superior to all powers within the State. 'A government', as he says, 'is not free to do as it pleases . . . the law of nature stands as an eternal rule to all men, legislators as well as others.' The social contract is secreted in the interstices of public statutes.

Its corollary is the right of revolution. It is interesting that he should have adopted this position; for in 1676 he had uttered the thought that not even the demands of conscience [1] can justify rebellion. That was, however, before the tyranny of Charles had driven him into exile with his patron, and before James had attempted the subversion of all constitutional government. To deny the right of revolution was to justify the worst demands of James, and it is in its favour that he exerts his ablest controversial power. 'The true remedy', he says, 'of force without authority is to oppose force to it.' Let

[1] King, *Life of Locke*, pp. 62, 63.

the sovereign but step outside the powers derived from
the social contract and resistance becomes a natural
right. But how define such invasion of powers? The
instances Locke chose show how closely, here at least,
he was following the events of 1688. The substitution of
arbitrary will for law, the corruption of Parliament by
packing it with the prince's instruments, betrayal to a
foreign prince, prevention of the due assemblage of
Parliament—all these are a perversion of the trust imposed and operate to effect the dissolution of the contract. The state of nature again supervenes, and a new
contract may be made with one more fitted to observe
it. Here, also, Locke takes occasion to deny the central
position of Hobbes's thesis. Power, the latter had argued,
must be absolute, and there cannot, therefore, be usurpation. But Locke retorts that an absolute government
is no government at all since it proceeds by caprice
instead of reason; and it is comparable only to a state
of war since it implies the absence of judgement upon
the character of power. It lacks the essential element of
consent without which the binding force of law is absent.
All government is a moral trust, and the idea of limitation is therein implied. But a limitation without the
means of enforcement would be worthless, and revolution
remains as the reserve power in society. The only
hindrance to its exertion that Locke suggests is that of
number. Revolution should not, he urges, be the act
of a minority; for the contract is the action of the major
portion of the people and its consent should likewise
obtain to the dissolution of the covenant.

The problem of Church and State demanded a separate
discussion; and it is difficult not to feel that the great
*Letter on Toleration* is the noblest of all his utterances. It

came as the climax to a long evolution of opinion; and,
in the light of William's own conviction, it may be said
to have marked a decisive epoch of thought. Already
in the sixteenth century Robert Brown and William the
Silent had denounced the persecution of sincere belief.
Early Baptists like Busher and Richardson had finely
denied its validity. Roger Williams in America, Milton
in England had attacked its moral rightness and political
adequacy; while churchmen like Hales and Taylor and
the noble Chillingworth had shown the incompatibility
between a religion of love and a spirit of hate. Nor had
example been wanting. The religious freedom of Holland
was narrow, as Spinoza had found, but it was still
freedom. Rhode Island, Pennsylvania, South Carolina,
and Massachusetts had all embarked upon admirable
experiment; and Penn himself had aptly said that a
man may go to chapel instead of church, even while
he remains a good constable. And in 1687, in the preface
to his translation of Lactantius, Burnet had not merely
attacked the moral viciousness of persecution, but had
drawn a distinction between the spheres of Church and
State which is a remarkable anticipation of Locke's own
theory.

Locke himself covers the whole ground; and since his
opinions on the problem were at least twenty years old
it is clear that he was consistent in a worthy outlook.
He proceeds by a denial that any element of theocratic
government can claim political validity. The magistrate
is concerned only with the preservation of social peace
and does not deal with the problem of men's souls.
Where, indeed, opinions destructive of the State are
entertained or a party subversive of peace makes its
appearance, the magistrate has the right of suppression;

though in the latter case force is the worst and last of
remedies. In the English situation, it follows that all
men are to be tolerated save Catholics, Mahomedans,
and atheists. The first are themselves deniers of the
rights they would seek, and they find the centre of their
political allegiance in a foreign power. Mahomedan
morals are incompatible with European civil systems;
and the central factor in atheism is the absence of the
only ultimately satisfactory sanction of good conduct.
Though Church and State are thus distinct, they act
for a reciprocal benefit; and it is thus important to see
why Locke insists on the invalidity of persecution. For
such an end as the cure of souls, he argues, the magistrate has no divine legation. He cannot, on other grounds,
use force for the simple reason that it does not produce
internal conviction. But even if that were possible, force
would still be mistaken; for the majority of the world
is not Christian, yet it would have the right to persecute
in the belief that it was possessed of truth. Nor can the
implication that the magistrate has the keys of heaven
be accepted. ' No religion ', says Locke finely, ' which
I believe not to be true can be either true or profitable
to me.' He thus makes of the Church an institution radi-
cally different from the ruling conceptions of his time.
It becomes merely a voluntary society, which can exert
no power save over its members. It may use its own
ceremonies, but it cannot impose them on the unwilling; and since persecution is alien from the spirit of
Christ, exclusion from membership must be the limit of
ecclesiastical disciplinary power. Nor must we forget
the advantages of toleration. Its eldest child is charity,
and without it there can be no honesty of opinion.
Later controversy did not make him modify these prin-

ciples; and they lived, in Macaulay's hands, to be a vital weapon in the political method of the nineteenth century.

## IV

Any survey of earlier political theory would show how little of novelty there is in the specific elements of Locke's general doctrine. He is at all points the offspring of a great and unbroken tradition; and that not the least when he seems unconscious of it. Definite teachers, indeed, he can hardly be said to have had; no one can read his book without perceiving how much of it is rooted in the problems of his own day. He himself has expressed his sense of Hooker's greatness, and he elsewhere had recommended the works of Grotius and Pufendorf as an essential element in education. But his was a nature which learned more from men than books; and he more than once insisted that his philosophy was woven of his own ' coarse thoughts '. What, doubtless, he therein meant was to emphasize the freshness of his contact with contemporary fact in contrast with the technical jargon of the earlier thinkers. At least his work is free from the mountains of allusion which Prynne rolled into the bottom of his pages; and if the first Whig was the devil, he is singularly free from the irritating pedantry of biblical citation. Yet even with these novelties, no estimate of his work would be complete which failed to take account of the foundations upon which he builded.

Herein, perhaps, the danger is lest we exaggerate Locke's dependence upon the earlier current of thought. The social contract is at least as old as when Glaucon debated with Socrates in the market-place at Athens. The theory of a state of nature, with the right therein implied, is the contribution, through Stoicism, of the Roman lawyers, and the great medieval contrast to Aristotle's experimentalism. To the latter, also, may be traced the separation of powers; and it was then but little more than a hundred years since Bodin had been taken to make the doctrine an integral part of scientific politics. Nor is the theory of a right to revolution in any sense his specific creation. So soon as the Reformation had given a new perspective to the problem of Church and State every element of Locke's doctrine had become a commonplace of debate. Goodman and Knox among Presbyterians, Suarez and Mariana among Catholics, the author of the *Vindiciæ* and Francis Hotman among the Huguenots, had all of them emphasized the concept of public power as a trust; with, of course, the necessary corollary that its abuse entails resistance. Algernon Sydney was at least his acquaintance; and he must have been acquainted with the tradition, even if tragedy spared him the details, of the *Discourses on Government*. Even his theory of toleration had in every detail been anticipated by one or other of a hundred controversialists; and his argument can hardly claim either the lofty eloquence of Jeremy Taylor or the cogent simplicity of William Penn.

What differentiates Locke from all his predecessors is the manner of his writing on the one hand, and the fact of the Revolution on the other. Every previous thinker save Sydney—the latter's work was not published until 1689—was writing with the Church hardly less in mind than the purely political problems of the State; even the secular Hobbes had devoted much thought and space to that 'kingdom of darkness' which is Rome. And, Sydney apart, the resistance they had justified was always resistance to a religious tyrant; and Cartwright was as careful to exclude political oppression from the grounds of revolution as Locke was to insist upon it as the fundamental excuse. Locke is, in fact, the first of English thinkers the basis of whose argument is mainly secular. Not, indeed, that he can wholly escape the trammels of ecclesiasticism; not until the sceptical intelligence of Hume was such freedom possible. But it is clear enough that Locke was shifting to very different ground from that which arrested the attention of his predecessors. He is attempting, that is to say, a separation between Church and State not merely in that Scoto-Jesuit sense which aimed at ecclesiastical independence, but in order to assert the pre-eminence of the State as such. The central problem is with him political, and all other questions are subsidiary to it. Therein we have a sense, less clear in any previous writer save Machiavelli, of the real result of the decay of medieval ideals. Church and State have become transposed in their significance. The way, as a consequence, lies open to new dogmas.

The historical research of the nineteenth century has long since made an end of the social contract as an explanation of state-origins; and with it, of necessity, has gone the conception of natural rights as anterior to organized society. The problem, as we now know, is far more complex than the older thinkers imagined. Yet Locke's insistence on consent and natural rights has received new meaning from each critical period of history since he wrote. The theory of consent is vital because without the provision of channels for its administrative expression, men tend to become the creatures of a power at once ignorant and careless of their will. Active consent on the part of the mass of men emphasizes the contingent nature of all power and is essential to the full realization of freedom; and the purpose of the State, in any sense save the mere satisfaction of material appetite, remains, without it, unfulfilled. The concept of natural right is most closely related to this position. For so long as we regard rights as no more than the creatures of law, there is at no point adequate safeguard against their usurpation. A merely legal theory of the State can never, therefore, exhaust the problems of political philosophy.

No thinker has seen this fact more clearly than Locke; and if his effort to make rights something more than interests under juridical protection cannot be accepted in the form he made it, the underlying purpose remains. A State, that is to say, which aims at giving to men the full capacity their trained initiative would permit is compelled to regard certain things as beyond the action of an ordinary legislature. What Stammler calls a 'natural law with changing content'[1]—a content which changes with our increasing power to satisfy demand—is essential if the State is to live the life of law. For here was the head and centre of Locke's inquiry. 'What he was really concerned about', said T. H. Green, 'was to dispute " the right divine of kings to govern wrong ".' The method, as he conceived, by which this could be accomplished was the limitation of power. This he effected by two distinct methods, the one external, the other internal in character.

The external method has, at bottom, two aspects.

[1] Cf. my *Authority in the Modern State*, p. 64, and the references there cited.

It is, in the first place, achieved by a narrow definition
of the purpose of the State. To Locke the State is little
more than a negative institution, a kind of gigantic
limited liability company; and if we are inclined to
cavil at such restraint, we may perhaps remember that
even to neo-Hegelians like Green and Bosanquet this
negative sense is rarely absent, in the interest of individual exertion. But for Locke the real guarantee of
right lies in another direction. What his whole work
amounts to in substance—it is a significant anticipation
of Rousseau—is a denial that sovereignty can exist
anywhere save in the community as a whole. A common political superior there doubtless must be; but
government is an organ to which omnipotence is wanting.
So far as there is a sovereign at all in Locke's book, it
is the will of that majority which Rousseau tried to
disguise under the name of the general will; but obviously the conception lacks precision enough to give
the notion of sovereignty the means of operation. The
denial is natural enough to a man who has seen, under
three sovereigns, the evils of unlimited power; and if
there is lacking to his doctrine the well-rounded logic
of Hobbes's proof that an unlimited sovereign is unavoidable, it is well to remember that the shift of opinion
is, in our own time, more and more in the direction of
Locke's attitude. That omnicompetence of Parliament
which Bentham and Austin crystallized into the retort
to Locke admits, in later hands, of exactly the ameliora-
tion he had in mind; and its ethical inadequacy becomes
the more obvious the more closely it is studied.[1]

The internal limitation Locke suggested is of more
doubtful value. Government, he says, in substance, is a

[1] Cf. my *Problem of Sovereignty*, Chapter I.

trustee and trustees abuse their power; let us therefore divide it as to parts and persons that the temptation to usurp may be diminished. There is a long history to this doctrine in its more obvious form, and it is a lamentable history. It tied men down to a tyrannous classification which had no root in the material it was supposed to distinguish. Montesquieu took it for the root of liberty; Blackstone, who should have known better, repeated the pious phrases of the Frenchman; and they went in company to America to persuade Madison and the Supreme Court of the United States that only the separation of powers can prevent the approach of tyranny. The facts do not bear out such assumption. The division of powers means in the event not less than their confusion. None can differentiate between the judge's declaration of law and his making of it.[1] Every government department is compelled to legislate, and, often enough, to undertake judicial functions. The American history of the separation of powers has most largely been an attempt to bridge them; and all that has been gained is to drive the best talent, save on rare occasion, from its public life. In France the separation of powers meant, until recent times, the excessive subordination of the judiciary to the Cabinet. Nor must we forget, as Locke should have remembered, the plain lesson of the Cromwellian constitutional experiments. That the dispersion of power is one of the great needs of the modern State at no point justifies the rigid categories into which Locke sought its division.[2]

Nor must we belittle the criticism, in its clearest form

---

[1] Cf. Justice Holmes's remarks in *Jensen* v. *Southern Pacific*, 244 U.S. 221.
[2] Cf. my *Authority in the Modern State*, pp. 70 f.

the work of Fitzjames Stephen,[1] that has been levelled
at Locke's theory of toleration. For the larger part of
the modern world, his argument is acceptable enough;
and its ingenious compromises have made it especially
representative of the English temper. Yet much of it
hardly meets the argument that some of his opponents,
as Proast for example, had made. His conception of the
visible church as no part of the essence of religion could
win no assent from even a moderate Anglican; and,
once the visible church is admitted, Locke's facile distinction between Church and State falls to the ground.
Nor can it be doubted that he underestimated the power
of coercion to produce assent; the policy of Louis XIV
to the Huguenots may have been brutal, but its efficacy
must be unquestionable. And it is at least doubtful
whether his theory has any validity for a man who held,
as Roman Catholics of his generation were bound to
hold, that the communication of his particular brand of
truth outweighed in value all other questions. ' Every
Church ', he wrote, ' is orthodox to itself; to others,
erroneous or heretical '; but to any earnest believer this
would approximate to blasphemy. Nor could any serious
Christian accept the view that ' under the gospel ". . .
there is no such thing as a Christian commonwealth " ';
to Catholics and Presbyterians this must have appeared
the merest travesty of their faith.

Here, indeed, as elsewhere Locke is the true progenitor
of Benthamism, and his work can hardly be understood
save in this context. Just as in his ethical inquiries it
was always the happiness of the individual that he
sought, so in his politics it was the happiness of the

[1] Cf. also Coleridge's apt remark. *Table Talk*, 3 January
1834.

subject he had in view. In each case it was to immediate experience that he made his appeal; and this perhaps explains the clear sense of a contempt for past tradition which pervades all his work. 'That which is for the public welfare', he said, 'is God's will'; and therein we have the root of that utilitarianism which, as Maine pointed out, is the real parent of all nineteenth-century change. And with Locke, as with the Benthamites, his clear sense of what utilitarianism demanded led to an over-emphasis of human rationalism. No one can read the second *Treatise* without perceiving that Locke looked upon the State as a machine which can be built and taken to pieces in very simple fashion. Herein, undoubtedly, he over-simplified the problem; and that made him miss some of the cardinal points a true psychology of the State must seize. His very contractualism, indeed, is part of this affection for the rational. It resulted in his failure to perceive how complex is the mass of motives embedded in the political act. The significance of herd instinct and the vast primitive deeps of the unconscious were alike hidden from him. All this is of defect; and yet excusably. For it needed the demonstration by Darwin of the kinship of man and beast for us to see the real substance of Aristotle's vision that man is embedded in political society.

## V

Once Locke's work had become known, its reputation was secure. Not, indeed, that it was entirely welcome to his generation. Men were not wanting who shrank from his thoroughgoing rationalism and felt that anything but reason must be the test of truth. Those who

stood by the ancient ways found it easy to discover republicanism and the roots of atheistic doctrine in his
work; and even the theories of Filmer could find defenders against him in the Indian summer of prerogative
under Queen Anne. John Hutton informed a friend
that he was not less dangerous than Spinoza; and the
opinion found an echo from the nonjuring sect. But
these, after all, were but the eddies of a stream fast
burying itself in the sands. For most, the Revolution was
a final settlement, and Locke was welcome as a writer
who had discovered the true source of political comfort.
So it was that William Molyneux could embody the ideas
of the 'incomparable treatise' in his demand for Irish
freedom; a book which, even in those days, occasioned
some controversy. Nor is it uninteresting to discover that
the translation of Hotman's *Franco-Gallia* should have
been embellished with a preface from one who, as
Molyneux wrote to Locke,[1] never met the Irish writer
without conversing of their common master. How
rapidly the doctrine spread we learn from a letter of
Bayle's in which, as early as 1693, Locke has already
become 'the gospel of the Protestants'. Nor was his
immediate influence confined to England. French Huguenots and the Dutch drew naturally upon so happy
a defender; and Barbeyrac, in the translation of Pufendorf which he published in 1706, cites no writer so often
as Locke. The speeches for the prosecution in the trial
of Sacheverell were almost wholesale adaptations of his
teaching; and even the accused counsel admitted the
legality of James's deposition in his speech for the defence.

More valuable testimony is not wanting. In the
*Spectator*, on six separate occasions, Addison speaks of

[1] Locke, *Works* (ed. of 1812), IX, 435.

him as one whose possession is a national glory. Defoe in his *Original Power of the People of England* made Locke the common possession of the average man, and offered his acknowledgements to his master. Even the malignant genius of Swift softened his hate to find the epithet ' judicious ' for one in whose doctrines he can have found no comfort. Pope summarized his teaching in the form that Bolingbroke chose to give it. Hoadly, in his *Original and Institution of Civil Government*, not only dismisses Filmer in a first part each page of which is modelled upon Locke, but adds a second section in which a defence of Hooker serves rather clumsily to conceal the care with which the second *Treatise* had also been pillaged. Even Warburton ceased for a moment his habit of belittling all rivals in the field he considered his own to call him, in that *Divine Legation* which he considered his masterpiece, ' the honour of this age and the instructor of the future '; but since Warburton's attack on the High Church theory is at every point Locke's argument, he may have considered this self-eulogy instead of tribute. Sir Thomas Hollis, on the eve of English Radicalism, published a noble edition of his book. And there is perhaps a certain humour in the remembrance that it was to Locke's economic tracts that Bolingbroke went for the arguments with which, in the *Craftsman*, he attacked the excise scheme of Walpole. That is irrefutable evidence of the position he had attained.

Yet the tide was already on the ebb, and for cogent reasons. There still remained the tribute to be paid by Montesquieu when he made Locke's separation of powers the keystone of his own more splendid arch. The most splendid of all sciolists was still to use his book for the

D

outline of a social contract more daring even than his
own. The authors of the *Declaration of Independence* had
still, in words taken from Locke, to reassert the state of
nature and his rights; and Mr. Martin of North Carolina
was to find him quotable in the debates of the Philadelphia Convention. Yet Locke's own weapons were
being turned against him and what was permanent in
his work was being cast into the new form required by
the time. A few sentences of Hume were sufficient to
make the social contract as worthless as the Divine
Right of kings, and when Blackstone came to sum up
the result of the Revolution, if he wrote in contractual
terms it was with a full admission that he was making
use of fiction so far as he went behind the settlement of
1688. Nor is the work of Dean Tucker without significance. The failure of England in the American war was
already evident; and it was not without justice that he
looked to Locke as the author of their principles. ' The
Americans ', he wrote, ' have made the maxims of Locke
the ground of the present war '; and in his *Treatise
Concerning Civil Government* and his *Four Letters* he declares
himself unable to understand on what Locke's reputation
was based. Meanwhile the English disciples of Rousseau
in the persons of Price and Priestley suggested to him
that Locke, ' the idol of the levellers of England ', was
the parent also of French destructiveness. Burke took up
the work thus begun; and after he had dealt with the
contract theory it ceased to influence political speculation
in England. Its place was taken by the utilitarian doctrine which Hume had outlined; and once Bentham's
*Fragment* had begun to make its way, a new epoch
opened in the history of political ideas.

Locke might, indeed, claim that he had a part in

this renaissance; but, once the influence of Burke had passed, it was to other gods men turned. For Bentham made an end of natural rights; and his contempt for the past was even more unsparing than Locke's own. It is more instructive to compare his work with Hobbes and Rousseau than with later thinkers; for after Hume English speculation works in a medium Locke would not have understood. Clearly enough, he has nothing of the relentless logic which made Hobbes's mind the clearest instrument in the history of English philosophy. Nor has he Hobbes's sense of style or pungent grasp of the grimness of facts about him. Yet he need not fear the comparison with the earlier thinker. If Hobbes's theory of sovereignty is to-day one of the commonplaces of jurisprudence, ethically and politically we occupy ourselves with erecting about it a system of limitations each one of which is in some sort due to Locke's perception. If we reject Locke's view of the natural goodness of men, Hobbes's sense of their evil character is not less remote from our speculations. Nor can we accept Hobbes's Erastianism. Locke's view of Church and State became, indeed, a kind of stepchild to it in the stagnant days of the later Georges; but Wesleyanism on the one hand, and the Oxford Movement on the other, pointed the inevitable moral of even an approximation to the Hobbesian view. And anyone who surveys the history of Church and State in America will be tempted to assert that in the last hundred years the separateness for which Locke contended is not without its justification. Locke's theory is a means of preserving the humanity of men; Hobbes makes their reason and conscience the subjects of a power he forbids them to judge. Locke saw that vigilance is the sister of liberty, where Hobbes dismissed the one as faction and the other as disorder. At every point, that is to say, where Hobbes and Locke are at variance, the future has been on Locke's side. He may have defended his cause less splendidly than his rival; but it will at least be admitted by most that he had a more splendid cause to defend.

With Rousseau there is no contrast, for the simple reason that his teaching is only a broadening of the channel dug by Locke. No element integral to the *Two Treatises* is absent from the *Social Contract*. Rousseau, indeed, in many aspects saw deeper than his predecessor. The form into which he threw his questions gave them an eternal significance Locke can perhaps hardly claim. He understood the organic character of the State, where Locke was still trammelled by the bonds of his narrow individualism. It is yet difficult to see that the contribution upon which Rousseau's fame has mainly rested is at any point a real advance upon Locke. The general will, in practical instead of semi-mystic terms, really means the welfare of the community as a whole; and when we inquire how that general will is to be known, we come, after much shuffling, upon the will of that majority in which Locke also put his trust. Rousseau's general will, indeed, is at bottom no more than an assertion that right and truth should prevail; and for this also Locke was anxious. But he did not think an infallible criterion existed for its detection; and he was satisfied with the convenience of a simple numerical test. Nor would it be difficult to show that Locke's state has more real room for individuality than Rousseau's. The latter made much show of an impartible and inalienable sovereignty eternally vested in the people; but in practice its exercise is impossible outside the confines of a city-state. Once, that is to say, we deal with modern problems our real inquiry is still the question of Locke —what limits shall we place upon the power of government? Rousseau has only emphasized the urgency of the debate.

Wherein, perhaps, the most profound distinction between Locke's teaching and our own time may be discovered is in our sense of the impossibility that a final answer can be found to political questions. Each age has new materials at its command; and, to-day, a static philosophy would condemn itself before completion. We do not build Utopias; and the attempt to discover the eternal principles of political right invites disaster at the outset. Yet that does not render useless, even for our own day, the kind of work Locke did. In the largest sense, his questions are still our own. In the largest sense, also, we are near enough to his time to profit at each step of our own efforts by the hints he proffers. The point at which he stood in English history bears not a little resemblance to our own. The emphasis, now as then, is upon the problem of freedom. The problem, now as then, was its translation into institutional terms. It is the glory of Locke that he brought a generous patience and a searching wisdom to the solution he proffered to his generation.

## CHAPTER III

# CHURCH AND STATE IN THE EIGHTEENTH CENTURY

## I

THE Revolution of 1688 drew its main source of strength from the traditional dislike of Rome, and the eager desire to place the Church of England beyond the reach of James's aggression. Yet it was not until a generation had passed that the lines of ecclesiastical settlement were, in any full sense, clear. The difficulties involved were mostly governmental, and it can hardly even yet be said that they have been solved. The nature of the relation between Church and State, the affiliation between the Church and Nonconformist bodies, the character of its internal government—all these had still to be defined. Nor was this all. The problem of definition was made more complex by schism and disloyalty. An important fraction of the Church could not accept at all the fact of William's kingship; and if the larger part submitted, it cannot be said to have been enthusiastic.

Nor did the Church make easy the situation of the Nonconformists. Toleration of some kind was rapidly becoming inevitable; and with a Calvinist upon the throne persecution of, at any rate, the Presbyterians became finally impossible. Yet the definition of what limits were to be set to toleration was far from easy. The Church seemed like a fortress beleaguered when

Nonjurors, Deists, Nonconformists, all alike assaulted her foundations. To loosen her hold upon political privilege seemed to be akin to self-destruction. And, after all, if Church and State were to stand in some connexion, the former must have some benefit from the alliance. Did such partnership imply exclusion from its privilege for all who could not accept the special brand of religious doctrine? Locke, at least, denied the assumption, and argued that since Churches are voluntary societies, they cannot and ought not to have reciprocal relation with the State. But Locke's theory was meat too strong for the digestion of his time; and no statesman would then have argued that a government could forego the advantage of religious support. And William, after all, had come to free the Church from her oppressor. Freedom implied protection, and protection in that age involved establishment. It was thus taken for granted by most members of the Church of England that her adoption by the State meant her superiority to every other form of religious organization. Superiority is by its nature exclusive, the more especially when it is united to a certainty of truth and a kinship with the dominant political interest of the time. Long years were thus to pass before the real meaning of the Toleration Act secured translation into more generous statutes.

The problem of the Church's government was hardly less complex. The very acerbity with which it was discussed proclaims that we are in an age of settlement. Much of the dispute, indeed, is doubtless due to the dislike of all High Churchmen for William; with their consequent unwillingness to admit the full meaning of his ecclesiastical supremacy. Much also is due to the fact that the bench of bishops, despite great figures like

Tillotson and Wake, was necessarily chosen for political
aptitude rather than for religious value. Nor did men
like Burnet and Hoadly, for all their learning, make
easy the path for brethren of more tender consciences.
The Church, moreover, must have felt her powers the
more valuable from the very strength of the assault to
which she was subjected. And the direct interference
with her governance implied by the Oaths of Allegiance
and of Abjuration raised questions we have not yet
solved. It suggested the subordination of Church to
State; and men like Hickes and Leslie were quick to
point out the Erastianism of the age. It is a fact inevitable in the situation of the English Church that the
charge of subjection to the State should rouse a deep
and quick resentment. She cannot be a Church unless
she is a *societas perfecta*; she cannot have within herself
the elements of perfect fellowship if what seem the plain
commands of Christ are to be at the mercy of the king
in Parliament. That is the difficulty which lies at the
bottom of the debate with Wake in one age and with
Hoadly in the next. In some sort, it is the problem of
sovereignty that is here at issue; and it is in this sense
that the problems of the Revolution are linked with the
Oxford Movement. But Newman and his followers are
the unconscious sponsors of a debate which grows in
volume; and to discuss the thoughts of Wake and Hoadly
and Law is thus, in a vital aspect, the study of contemporary ideas.

We are not here concerned with the wisdom of those
of William's advisers who exacted an oath of allegiance
from the clergy. It raised in acute form the validity of
a doctrine which had, for more than a century, been
the main foundation of the alliance between throne

and altar in England. The demand precipitated a schism which lingered on, though fitfully, until the threshold of the nineteenth century. The men who could not take the oath were, many of them, among the most distinguished churchmen of the time. Great ecclesiastics like Sancroft, the Archbishop of Canterbury and one of the seven who had gained immortality by his resistance to James, saints like Ken, the Bishop of Bath and Wells, scholars like George Hickes and Henry Dodwell, men like Charles Leslie, born with a genius for recrimination; much, it is clear, of what was best in the Church of England was to be found amongst them. There is not a little of beauty, and much of pathos in their history. Most, after their deprivation, were condemned to poverty; few of them recanted. The lives of men like Sancroft and Ken and the younger Ambrose Bonwicke are part of the great Anglican tradition of earnest simplicity which later John Keble was to illustrate for the nineteenth century. The Nonjurors, as they were called, were not free from bitterness; and the history of their effort, after the consecration of Hilkiah Bedford and Ralph Taylor, to perpetuate the schism is a lamentable one. Not, indeed, that the history even of their decline is without its interest; and the study, alike of their liturgy and their attempt at reunion with the Eastern Church, must always possess a singular interest for students of ecclesiastical history.

Yet the real interest of the Nonjuring schism was political rather than religious; and its roots go out to vital events of the past. At the bottom it is the obverse side of the Divine Right of kings that they represent. That theory, which was the main weapon of the early secular State against the pretensions of Rome, must naturally have commanded the allegiance of members of a Church which James I, its main exponent, had declared of vital import to his very existence. Its main opponents, moreover, were Catholics and Dissenters; so that men like Andrewes must have felt that when they answered Bellarmine they were in substance also defenders of their Church. After the great controversy of James I's reign resistance as a duty had come to be regarded as a main element in Jesuit and Nonconformist teaching; with the result that its antithesis became, as a consequence of the political situation, no less integral a part of Church of England doctrine. For it was upon the monarchy that the Church had come to depend for its existence; and if resistance to the king were made, as Knox and Bellarmine had in substance made it, the main weapon of the dissenting Churches, there was little hope that it would continue to exist once the monarchy was overthrown. And it is this, unquestionably, which explains why stout ecclesiastics like Barrow and Jackson can write in what seems so Erastian a temper. When they urge the sovereignty of the State, their thesis is in truth the sovereignty of the Church; and that means the triumph of men who looked with contemptuous hatred upon Nonconformists of every sect. The Church of England taught non-resistance as the condition of its own survival.

How deep-rooted this doctrine had become in the course of the seventeenth century the writings of men like Mainwaring and Sanderson sufficiently show; yet nothing so completely demonstrates its widespread acceptance as the result of the Revolution. Four hundred clergy abandoned their preferment because James ruled by Divine Right; and they could not in conscience resist even his iniquities. An able tract of 1689 [1] had collected much material to show how integral the doctrine was to the beliefs of the Church. Had William's government, indeed, refrained from the imposition of the oath, it is possible that there might have been no schism at all; for the early Nonjurors at least—perhaps Hickes and Turner are exceptions—would probably have welcomed anything which enabled the avoidance of schism. Once, however, the oath was imposed three vital questions were raised. Deprivation obviously involved the problem of the power of the State over the Church. If the act of a convention whose own legality was at best doubtful could deprive the consecrated of their position, was the Church a Church at all, or was it the mere creature of the secular power? And what, moreover, of conscience? It could not be an inherent part of the Church's belief that men should betray their faith for the sake of peace. Later thinkers added the purely secular argument that resistance in one case made for resistance in all. Admit, it was argued by Leslie, the right to disobey, and the fabric of society is at a stroke dissolved. The attitude is characteristic of that able controversialist; and it shows how hardly the earlier notions of Divine Right were to die.

These theories merit a further examination. Williams, later the Bishop of Chichester, had argued that separation on the basis of the oath was unreasonable. ' All that the civil power here pretends to ', he wrote, ' is to secure itself against the practices of dissatisfied persons.' The Nonjurors, in this view, were making an ecclesiastical matter of a purely secular issue. He was answered,

[1] *The History of Passive Obedience.* Its author was Jeremy Collier.

among others, by Samuel Grascom, in an argument
which found high favour among the stricter of his sect.
'The matter and substance of these Oaths', he said,
'is put into the prayers of the Church, and so far it
becomes a matter of communion. What people are en-
joined in the solemn worship to pray for, is made a
matter of communion; and if it be simple, will not only
justify, but require a separation.' Here is the pith of
the matter. For if the form and substance of Church
affairs is thus to be left to governmental will, then those
who obey have left the Church and it is the faithful
remnant only who constitute the true fellowship. The
schism, in this view, was the fault of those who remained
subject to William's dominion. The Nonjurors had not
changed; and they were preserving the Church in its
integrity from men who strove to betray it to the civil
power.

This matter of integrity is important. The glamour
of Macaulay has somewhat softened the situation of
those who took the oaths; and in his pages the Nonjurors appear as stupid men unworthily defending a
dead cause. It is worth while to note that this is the
merest travesty. Tillotson, who succeeded Sancroft on
the latter's deprivation, and Burnet himself had urged
passive resistance upon Lord William Russell as essential
to salvation; Tenison had done likewise at the execution
of Monmouth. Stillingfleet, Patrick, White Kennett,
had all written in its favour; and to William Sherlock
belongs the privilege of having defended and attacked
it in two pamphlets each of which challenges the pithy
brilliance of the other. Clearly, so far as consistency is
in question, the Nonjurors might with justice contend
that they had right on their side. And even if it is said

that the policy of James introduced a new situation the answer surely is that Divine Right and non-resistance can, by their very nature, make no allowance for novelty.

The root, then, of this ecclesiastical contention is the argument later advanced by Leslie in his ' Case of the Regale and the Pontificate ' in which he summarized the Convocation dispute. The State, he argues, has no power over bishops, whose relationship to their flock is purely spiritual and derived from Christ. The Church is independent of all civil institution, and must have therefore within herself the powers necessary to her life as a society. Leslie repudiates Erastianism in the strongest terms. Not only is it, for him, an encroachment upon the rights of Christ, but it leads to deism in the gentry and to dissent among the common people. The Church of England comes to be regarded as no more than the creature of Parliamentary enactment; and thus to leave it as the creature of human votes is to destroy its divinity.

It is easy enough to see that men who felt in this fashion could hardly have decided otherwise than as they did. The matter of conscience, indeed, was funda-mental to their position. ' I think ', said the Bishop of Worcester on his death-bed, ' I could suffer at a stake rather than take this oath.' That, indeed, represents the general temper. Many of them did not doubt that James had done grievous wrong; but they had taken the oath of allegiance to him, and they saw in their conscience no means of escape from their vow. ' Their Majesties ', writes the author of the account of Bishop Lake's death, ' are the two persons in the world whose reign over them, their interest and inclination oblige them most to desire, and nothing but conscience could

restrain them from being as forward as any in all ex-
pressions of loyalty.' In such an aspect, even those who
believe their attitude to have been wrong, can hardly
doubt that they acted rightly in their expression of it. For,
after all, experience has shown that the State is built
upon the consciences of men. And the protest they
·made stands out in the next generation in vivid contrast
to a wordly-minded and politically-corrupt Church
which only internal revolution could awaken from its
slumbers.

No one represents so admirably as Charles Leslie the
political argument of the case. At bottom it is an argument against anarchy that he constructs, and much of
what he said is medieval enough in tone to suggest de
Maistre's great defence of papalism as the secret of
world-order. He stands four square upon Divine Right
and passive obedience. ' What man is he who can by
his own natural authority bend the conscience of another? That would be far more than the power of life,
liberty or prosperity. Therefore they saw the necessity
of a divine original.' Such a foundation, he argued
elsewhere, is necessary to order, for ' if the last resort
be in the people, there is no end of controversy at all,
but endless and unremediable confusion '. Nor had he
sympathy for the Whig attack on monarchy. ' The
reasons against Kings ', he wrote, ' are as strong against
all powers, for men of any titles are subject to err, and
numbers more than fewer.' And nothing can unloose the
chain. ' Obedience ', he said in the *Best of All*, ' is due
to commonwealths by their subjects even for conscience'
sake, where the princes from whom they have revolted
have given up their claim.'

The argument has a wider history than its controversial statement might seem to warrant. At bottom, clearly enough, it is an attack upon the new tradition which Locke had brought into being. What seems to impress it most is the impossibility of founding society upon other than a divine origin. Anything less will not command the assent of men sufficiently to be immune from their evil passions. Let their minds but once turn to resistance, and the bonds of social order will be broken. Complete submission is the only safeguard against anarchy. So, a century later, de Maistre could argue that unless the whole world became the subject of Rome, the complete dissolution of Christian society must follow. So, too, fifty years before, Hobbes had argued for an absolute dominion lest the ambitions and desires of men break through the fragile boundaries of the social estate.

The answer is clear enough; and, indeed, the case against the Nonjurors is nowhere so strong as on its political side. Men cannot be confined within the limits of so narrow a logic. They will not, with Bishop Ken, rejoice in suffering as a doctrine of the Cross. Rather will oppression in its turn arouse a sense of wrong and that be parent of a conscience which provokes to action. Here was the root of Locke's doctrine of consent; for unless the government, as Hume was later to point out, has on its side the opinion of men, it cannot hope to endure. The fall of James was caused not, as the Nonjurors were tempted to think, by popular disregard of Divine personality, but by his own misunderstanding of the limits to which misgovernment may go. Here their opponents had a strong case to present; for, as Stillingfleet remarked, if William had not come over there might have been no Church of England for the Nonjurors to preserve. And other ingenious compromises

were suggested. Non-resistance, it was argued by Sherlock, applied to government in general; and the oath,
as a passage in the *Convocation Book* of Overall seemed
to suggest, might be taken not less to a *de facto* monarch
than to one *de jure*. Few, indeed, would have taken the
ground of Bishop Burnet, and allotted the throne to
William and Mary as conquerors of the kingdom; at
least the pamphlet in which this uncomfortable doctrine
was put forward the House of Commons had burned by
the common hangman.

What really defeated the Nonjurors' claims was
common sense. Much the ablest attack upon their
position was Stillingfleet's defence of the policy em-
ployed in filling up the sees vacated by deprivation;
and it is remarkable that the theory he employs is to
insist that unless the lawfulness of what had been done
is admitted, the Nonjurors' position is inevitable. ' If it
be unlawful to succeed a deprived bishop,' he wrote,[1]
' then he is the bishop of the diocese still: and then the
law that deprives him is no law, and consequently the
king and Parliament that made that law no king and
Parliament: and how can this be reconciled with the
Oath of Allegiance, unless the Doctor can swear
allegiance to him who is no King and hath no authority
to govern.' All this the Nonjurors would have admitted,
and the mere fact that it could be used as argument
against them is proof that they were out of touch with
the national temper. What they wanted was a legal
revolution, which is in the nature of things impossible.
We may regret that the oath was deemed essential, and
feel that it might not have been so stoutly pressed.

[1] *A Vindication of their Majesties' Authority to fill the Sees of
the Deprived Bishops* (1691).

But the leaders of a revolution ' tread a path of fire ';
and the fault lay less at the door of the civil government
than in the fact that this was an age when men acted
on their principles. William and his advisers, with the
condition of Ireland and Scotland a cause for agitation,
with France hostile, with treason and plot not absent
from the episcopate itself, had no easy task; what, in
the temper of the time, gives most cause for consideration
is the moderate spirit in which they accomplished it.

## II

The Nonjuring schism was by no means the only
difficulty which the Church of England had to confront
in these troubled years. The definition of her relationship with State and nation, if at the moment it aroused
less bitterness, was in the long run more intricate in its
nature. That some sort of toleration was inevitable few,
save a group of prejudiced irreconcilables, would have
denied. But greater things were in the air, and there
were still many who dreamed of a grand scheme of Com-
prehension, by which all save the more extreme Dissenters would have been admitted to the Church. It is
this which explains the acrimonious debates of the next
two years. The hatred of the Church for dissent can
only be understood by those who study with care the
insults heaped upon her by the sectaries during the
Civil Wars. That men who had striven for her dissolution
should be admitted to her privileges seemed to churchmen as tragic as ironical. Nor must we miss the political
aspect of the matter. William had received an eager,
if natural, support from Nonconformists; and since the
vast majority of them was Whig in temper, the greater

E

the degree of toleration, the greater likelihood there was of an attack upon the Church. Exclusion thus became a fundamental article of the Tory creed; and it was the more valued because it enabled them to strike at their opponents through an institution which at the trial of Sacheverell, in 1710, still showed an overwhelming hold upon the mass of the people.

The attitude of mind herein implied is in large part the reaction from the Erastian temper of the government. Under William, that temper is intelligible enough; for unless he held the Church in strict control, he must have felt that he was giving a large handle to his enemies. Under Anne, the essence of the situation remained unchanged, even though her eager sympathy with the Church was beyond all question. William had relieved Nonconformists from the burden of penal statute; the Occasional Conformity Act of 1713 broadly continued the exclusion of all save the more yielding of them from political office. When the Hanoverians succeeded they were willing to repeal its more rigid intolerance; but the Test Act remained as evidence that the Dissenters were not yet regarded as in a full sense part of the national life.

The reasons for the hatred of dissent go back in part to the Civil War and in part also to the feeling of common ground between the dissenting interest and Rome which was born of the struggle under Elizabeth and James. The pamphlets are innumerable; and most of them deserve the complete oblivion into which they have fallen. We are told, in the eighteenth as in the seventeenth century, that the Presbyterian theory of government is inconsistent with the existence of the civil power. 'They claim', said Leslie, 'power to abrogate the laws of the land touching ecclesiastical matters, if they judge them hurtful or unprofitable. . . . They require the civil magistrate to be subject to their power.' Of Knox or Cartwright this is no unfair account; but of the later Presbyterians it is the merest travesty. It supposes that they would be willing to push to the utmost limit the implications of the theory of the two kingdoms—a supposition which their passive submission to the Act of 1712 restoring lay patronage decisively refutes. Bramhall had no doubt that their discipline was ' the very quintessence of refined popery ', and the argument is repeated by a hundred less learned pamphleteers. Neither the grim irony of Defoe nor the proven facts of the case could wean either the majority of churchmen or the masses of the people from the belief that the Revolution endangered the very existence of the Church and that concession would be fatal. So stoutly did the Church resist it that the accession of George I alone, in Lecky's view, prevented the repeal of the Toleration Act and the destruction of the political benefits of the Revolution.

But nowhere was the temper of the time more clearly displayed than in the disputes over Convocation. To William's advisers, perhaps, more than to the Church itself their precipitation is due; for had they not, at the outset of the reign, suggested large changes in the liturgy suspicions then aroused might well have slumbered. As it was, the question of the royal supremacy immediately came into view and the clergy spared no effort to meet the issue so raised. And this they felt the more bitterly because the upper house of Convocation, two-thirds of which were William's nominees, naturally inclined to his side. Both under William and Anne the dispute continued, and the lower clergy shrank from no opportunity of conflict. They fought the king, the arch-bishop, the upper house. They attacked the writings of Toland and Burnet, the latter's book since recognized as one of the great treasures of Anglican literature. In the main, of course, the struggle was part of the perennial conflict between High Church doctrine and latitudina-rianism. But that was only a fragment of the issue. What really was in question was the nature of the State's power over the Church. That could be left unanswered so long as with James I and Charles, the two powers had but a single thought. The situation changed only when State and Church had different policies to fulfil and different means for their attainment.

The controversy had begun on the threshold of William's accession; but its real commencement dates from 1697. In that year was published the *Letter to a Convocation Man*, probably written by Sir Bartholomew Shower, an able if unscrupulous Jacobite lawyer, which maliciously, though with abounding skill, raised every question that peaceful churchmen must have been anxious to avoid. The *Letter* pointed out the growth of infidelity and the increasing suspicion that the Church was becoming tainted with Socinian doctrine. Only the assembly of Convocation could arrest these evils. The author did not deny that the king's assent was necessary to its summons. But he argued that once the Convocation had met, it could, like Parliament, debate all questions relevant to its purpose. ' The one of these courts ', said Shower, ' is of the same power and use with regard to the Church as the other is in respect to the State ', and he insisted that the writ of summons could not at any point confine debate. And since the Convocation was an

ecclesiastical Parliament, it followed that it could legislate and thus make any canons 'provided they do not
impugn common law, statutes, customs or prerogative'.
'To confer, debate and resolve', said Shower, 'without
the king's license, is at common law the undoubted
right of convocation.'

Here was a clear challenge which was at once answered, in *The Authority of Christian Princes*, by William
Wake, who was by far the most learned of the latitudinarian clergy and the successor of Tenison in the
see of Canterbury. His argument was purely historical.
He endeavoured to show that the right to summon
ecclesiastical synods was always the prerogative of the
early Christian princes until the aggression of the popes
had won church independence. The Reformation re-
sumed the primitive practice; and the Act of Submission
of 1532 had made it legally impossible for the clergy to
discuss ecclesiastical matters without royal permission.
Historically, the argument of Wake was irrefutable; but
what mostly impressed the Church was the uncompromising Erastianism of his tone. Princes, he said,
'may make what laws or constitutions they think fit
for the Church . . . a canon is but as matter prepared
for the royal stamp'. In this view, obviously, the Church
is no more than a department of the State. But Wake went
even farther: 'I cannot see why the Supreme Magistrate', he wrote, 'who confessedly has a power to
confirm or reject their [Convocation's] decrees, may not
also make such other use of them as he pleases, and cor-
rect, improve, or otherwise alter their resolutions,
according to his own liking, before he gives his authority
to them.'

So defined, no Church could claim in any true sense

the headship of Christ; for it was clearly left at the mercy of the governmental view of expedient conduct. Wake's answer aroused a sensation almost as acute as the original *Letter* of Shower. But by far the ablest criticism it provoked was that of Francis Atterbury, then a young student of Christ Church and on the threshold of his turbulent career. His *Rights, Powers and Privileges of an English Convocation Stated and Vindicated* not only showed a masterly historic sense in its effort to traverse the unanswerable induction of Wake, but challenged his position more securely on the ground of right. The historical argument, indeed, was not a safe position for the Church, and Wake's rejoinder in his *State of the Church* (1703) is generally conceded to have proved his point, so far as the claim of prescription is concerned. But when Atterbury moves to the deeper problem of what is involved in the nature of a Church, he has a powerful plea to make. It is unnecessary to deal with his contention that Wake's defence of the Royal Supremacy undermines the rights of Parliament; for Wake could clearly reply that the seat of that power had changed with the advent of the Revolution. Where the avoidance of sympathy is difficult is in his insistence that no Church can live without an assembly to debate its problems, and that no assembly can be real which is subject to external control. ' Their body ', as he remarks, ' will be useless to the State and by consequence contemptible '; for its opinions will not be born of that free deliberation which can alone ensure respect. Like all High Churchmen, Atterbury has a clear sense that Church and State can no longer be equated, and he is anxious to preserve the personality of the Church from the invasions of an alien body. To be real, it must be independent, and to be independent, it must have organs of self-expression. But neither William nor Anne could afford to forego the political capital involved in ecclesiastical control, and Erastian principles proceeded to their triumph.

Here, as elsewhere, it was Charles Leslie who best summed up the feeling of High Churchmen. His *Case of the Regale* (1701) is by far the ablest of his many able performances. He saw at the outset that the real issue was defined by the Church's claim to be a divine society, with rights thus consecrated by the conditions of its origin. If it was divine, invasion did not touch its *de jure* rights. ' How ', he asked, ' can rights that are divine be given up? If they are divine, no human authority can either supersede or limit them. . . . How can rights that are inherent be given up? If they are inherent, they are inseparable. The right to meet, to consult, to make rules or canons for the regulation of the society, is essential to every society as such . . . can she then part with what is essential to her?' Nor could it be denied that ' where the choice of the governors of one society is in the hands of another society, that society must be dependent and subject to the other '. The Church, in the latitudinarian view, was thus either the creature of the State or an *imperium in imperio*; but Leslie would not admit that fruitful stumbling-block to the debate. ' The sacred and civil powers were like two parallel lines which could never meet or interfere . . . the confusion arises . . . when the civil power will take upon them to control or give laws to the Church, in the exercise of her spiritual authority.' He did not doubt that the Church should give securities for its loyalty to the king, and renounce any effort at the coercion of the civil magistrate. But the Church was entitled to a similar privilege, and kings should not ' have their beneficence and protection to the Church of Christ understood as a bribe to her, to betray and deliver up into their hands the powers committed into her charge by Christ '. Nor did he fail to point out the suicidal nature of Erastianism. For the Church's hold upon men is dependent upon their faith in the independence of her principles. ' When they see bishops ', he wrote wisely, ' made by the Court, they are apt to imagine that they speak to them the court language; and lay no further stress upon it than the charge of a judge at an assizes, who has received his instructions beforehand from the Court; and by this means the state has lost the greatest security of her government.'

The argument is powerful enough; though it should be noted that some of its implications remain undetermined. Leslie does not say how the spheres of Church and State are to be differentiated. He does not explain the methods whereby an establishment is to be made compatible with freedom. For it is obvious that the partnership of Church and State must be upon conditions; and once the State had permitted the existence of creeds other than that of its official adoption, it could not maintain the exclusive power for which the Church contended. And when the Church not only complained of State-betrayal, but attempted the use of political means to enforce remedial measures, it was inevitable that statesmen would use the weapons ready to their hand to coerce it to their will. The real remedy for the High Churchmen was not exclusiveness but disestablishment.

That this is the meaning of the struggle did not

appear until the reign of George I. What is known as
the Bangorian controversy was due to the posthumous
publication, in 1716, of the papers of George Hickes,
the most celebrated of the Nonjurors in his generation.
The papers are of no special import; but taken in
connexion with the Jacobite rising of 1715 they seemed
to imply a new attack upon the Revolution settlement.
So, at least, they were interpreted by Benjamin Hoadly,
then Bishop of Bangor, and a stout upholder of the
latitudinarian school. The conflict to-day has turned to
dust and ashes; and few who read the multitude of
pamphlets it evoked, or stand amazed at their personal
bitterness, can understand why more than a hundred
writers should have thought it necessary to inform the
world of their opinions, or why the London Stock
Exchange should have felt so passionate an interest in
the debate as to cease for a day the hubbub of its transac-
tions. Nor can anyone make heroes from the personalities
of its protagonists. Hoadly himself was a typical bishop
of the political school, who rose from humble circumstances to the wealthy bishopric of Winchester through
a remarkable series of translations. Before the debate of
1716, he was chiefly known by two political tracts in
which he had rewritten, in less cogent form and without
adequate acknowledgement, the two treatises of Locke.
He clearly realized how worthless the dogma of Divine
Right had become, without being certain of the principles by which it was to be replaced. Probably, as
Leslie Stephen has pointed out, his theorizing is the
result of a cloudy sense of the bearing of the Deist controversy. If God is to be banished from direct connexion
with earthly affairs, we must seek a human explanation
of political facts. And he became convinced that this

attitude applies not less completely to ecclesiastical than
to secular politics. Of his opponents, by far the ablest
was William Law, the only theologian whom Gibbon
may be said to have respected, and the parent, through
his mystical writings, of the Wesleyan movement. Snape,
then Provost of Eton, was always incisive; and his pamphlet went through seventeen editions in a single year
and provoked seven replies within three months. Thomas
Sherlock would not be either himself or his father's son
were he not caustic, logical, and direct. But Hoadly
and Law between them exhaust the controversy, so far
as it has meaning for our own day. The less essential
questions, like Hoadly's choice of friends, his attitude to
prayer, the accuracy of the details in his account of the
Test Act, the cause of his refusal to answer Law directly,
are hardly now germane to the substance of the debate.
Hoadly's position is most fully stated in his *Preservative
against the Principles and Practice of Nonjurors* which he
published in 1716 as a counterblast to the papers of
Hickes; and they are briefly summarized in the sermon
preached before the king on 31 March 1717, on the
text ' My Kingdom is not of this world ', and published
by royal command. Amid a vast wilderness of quibbles
and qualifications, some simple points emerge. What he
was doing was to deprive the priesthood of claims to
supernatural authority that he might vindicate for civil
government the right to preserve itself not less against
persons in ecclesiastical office than against civil assailants.
To do so he is forced to deny that the miraculous powers
of Christ and the apostles descended to their successors.
For if that assumption is made we grant to fallible men
privileges which confessedly belong to persons outside
the category of fallibility. And, exactly in the fashion

of Leslie in the *Regale*, he goes on to show that if a Church is a supernatural institution, it cannot surrender one jot or tittle of its prerogative. It is, in fact, an *imperium in imperio* and its conflict with the State is inevitable. But if the Church is not a supernatural institution, what is its nature? Hoadly here attacks the doctrine which lies at the basis of all ecclesiastical debate. The Church, he claims, is not a visible society, presided over by men who have authority directly transmitted by Christ. There are not within it ' viceregents who can be said properly to supply his place; no interpreters upon whom his subjects are absolutely to depend; no judges over the conscience or religion of his people. For if this were so that any such absolute viceregent authority, either for the making of new laws, or interpreting old ones, or judging his subjects, in religious matters, were lodged in any men upon earth, the consequence would be that what still retains the name of the Church of Christ would not be the kingdom of Christ, but the kingdom of those men invested with such authority. For whoever hath such an authority of making laws is so far a king, and whoever can add new laws to those of Christ, equally obligatory, is as truly a king as Christ himself. Nay, whosoever hath an absolute authority to interpret any written or spoken laws, it is he who is truly the lawgiver to all intents and purposes, and not the person who first wrote and spoke them.'

The meaning is clear enough. What Hoadly is attacking is the theory of a visible Church of Christ on earth, with the immense superstructure of miracle and infallibility erected thereon. The true Church of Christ is in heaven; and the members of the earthly society can but try in a human, blundering way to act with decency and justice. Apostolic succession, the power of excommunication, the dealing out of forgiveness for men's sins, the determination of true doctrine—in so far as the Church claims these powers, it is usurping an authority that is not its own. The relation of man to God is his private affair, and God will ask from him sincerity and honesty, rather than judge him for possession of some special set of dogmas. Clearly, therefore, if the Church is no more than this, it has no supernatural pretensions to oppose to the human claims of the State. And since the State must have within itself all the means of sufficient life, it has the right to resist the ecclesiastical onslaught as based upon the usurpation of power assumed without right. And in the later treatises Hoadly did for ceremonial exactly what he had done for church government. The eucharist became a piece of symbolism and excommunication nothing more than an announcement—' a mere external thing '—that the rules of the fellowship have been broken. It at no point is related to the sinner's opportunity of salvation.

In such an aspect, it would clearly follow that the Church has no monopoly of truth. It can, indeed, judge its own beliefs; but reason alone can demonstrate the inadequacy of other attitudes. Nor does its judgement preclude the individual duty to examine into the truth of things. The real root of faith is not the possession of an infallible dogma, but the arriving honestly at the dogma in which you happen to believe. For the magistrate, he urges, what is important is not the table of your springs of action, but the conduct itself which is based upon that table; from which it follows that things like the Test and Corporation Acts have no real political validity. They have been imposed upon the State by the narrow interpretations of a usurping power; and the Nonconformist claim to citizenship would thus seem as valid as that of a member of the Church of England.

All this sounds sensible enough; though it is curious doctrine in the mouth of a bishop of that Church. And this, in fact, is the starting-point of Law's analysis of Hoadly. No one who reads the unsparing vigour of his criticism can doubt that Law must have been thoroughly happy in the composition of his defence; and, indeed, his is the only contribution to the debate which may claim a permanent place in political literature. In one sense, indeed, the whole of Law's answer is an *ignoratio elenchi*, for he assumes the truth of that which Hoadly sets out to examine, with the inevitable result that each writer is, for the most part, arguing from different premisses. But on the assumption that Hoadly is a Christian, Law's argument is an attack of great power. He shows conclusively that if the Church of England is no more than Hoadly imagines it to be, it cannot, in any proper historic sense, be called the Church of England at all. For every one of the institutions which Hoadly calls a usurpation is believed by churchmen to be integral to its nature. And if sincerity alone is to count as the test, then there cannot, for the existing world, be any such thing as objective religious truth. It subverted not merely absolute authority—which the Church of England did not claim—but any authority in the Church. It impugned the authority of the Crown to enforce religious belief by civil penalties. Hoadly's rejection of authority, moreover, is in Law's view fatal to government of any kind. For all lawful authority must affect eternal salvation in so far as to disobey it is to sin. The authority the Church possesses is inherent in the very nature of the Church; for the obligation to a belief in Christianity is the same thing as to a belief in that Church which can be shown to represent Christ's teaching.

From Law's own point of view, the logic of his position is undeniable; and in his third letter to Hoadly, the real heart of his attack, he touches the centre of the latter's argument. For if it is sincerity which is alone important it would follow that things false and wrong are as acceptable to God as things true and right, which is patently absurd. Nor has Hoadly given us means for the detection of sincerity. He seemed to think that anyone was sincere who so thought himself; but, says Law, ' it is also possible and as likely for a man to be mistaken in those things which constitute true sincerity as in those things which constitute true religion'. Clearly, sincerity cannot be the pith of the matter; for it may be mistaken and directed to wrong ends. The State, in fact, may respect conscience, but Hoadly is no more entitled to assume the infallibility of private belief than he is to deny the infallibility of the Church's teaching. That way lies anarchy.

Here, indeed, the antagonists were on common ground. Both had denied the absolute character of any authority; but while Hoadly virtually postulates a Church which logically is no more than those who accept the moral law as Christ described it, Law restricts the Church to that society which bears the traditional marks of the historic institution. On Hoadly's principles, there was no reason why anyone not hostile to the civil power should not enjoy political privilege; on Law's there was every reason simply because those who denied the doctrines of the High Church refused a truth open for

their acceptance. Law, indeed, goes so far as to argue
that in the light of his principles Hoadly should be a
Deist; and there is ground for what, in that age, was a
valuable point to make. The sum total of it all is that
for the Bishop the outward actions of men alone concern
the State; while Law insists that the root of action and
the test of fitness is whether men have seen a certain
aspect of the truth and grasped it.

The result, to say the least, was calamitous. In May
of 1717, Convocation met and the lower house immediately adopted a unanimous report condemning the
' Preservative ' and the sermon. But Hoadly had the
government behind him and the Convocation was pro-
rogued before further action could be taken. Snape,
Hare, Mosse, and Sherlock, all of whom were chaplains-
royal, and had been drawn into the conflict, were dismissed from their office; and for more than one hundred
and thirty-five years Convocation was not again sum-
moned. It was a striking triumph for Erastianism,
though the more liberal principles of Hoadly were less
successful. Robert Walpole was on the threshold of his
power, and, as a manager of Sacheverell's impeachment,
he had seen the hold of the Church upon the common
people, may even, indeed, have remembered that
Hoadly's own dwelling had been threatened with destruction in the popular excitement. *Quieta non movere*
was his motto; and he was not interested in the niceties
of ecclesiastic metaphysic. So the Test Act remained
immovable until 1828; while the annual Act of Indem-
nity for its infractions represented that English genius
for illogical mitigation which solves the deeper problems
of principle while avoiding the consideration of their
substance.

In the hundred and twenty years which passed between the Bangorian Controversy and the Oxford Movement, there is only one volume upon the problem of Church and State which deserves more than passing notice. Bishop Warburton was the Lord Brougham of his age; and as its self-constituted universal provider of intellectual fare, he deemed it his duty to settle this, amongst others, of the eternal questions. The effort excited only the contempt of Leslie Stephen—'the peculiar Warburton mixture', he says, 'of sham logic and bluster'. Yet that is hardly fair to the total result of Warburton's remarks. He tried to steer a middle path between the logical result of such Erastianism as that of the *Independent Whig*, on the one hand, and the excessive claim of High Churchmanship on the other. Naturally enough, or the writer would not be Warburton, the book is full of tawdry rhetoric and stupid quibbles. But the *Alliance between Church and State* (1736) set the temper of speculation until the advent of Newman, and is therefore material for something more than contempt. It acutely points out that societies generate a personality distinct from that of their members, in words reminiscent of an historic legal pronouncement.[1] ' When any number of men ', he says, ' form themselves into a society, whether civil or religious, this society becomes a body different from that aggregate which the number of individuals composed before the society was formed. . . . But a body must have its proper personality and will, which without these is no more than a shadow or a name.'

And that is the root of Warburton's pronouncement. The Church is a society distinct from the State, but lending to that body its assistance because without the

[1] Dicey, *Law and Opinion in England* (2nd edition), p. 165.

sanction of religion the full achievement of the social purpose is impossible. There is thus an alliance between them, each lending its support to the other for their common benefit. The two remain distinct; the union between them is of a federal kind. But they interchange their powers, and this it is which explains at once the royal supremacy and the right of churchmen to a share in the legislature. This also it is which explains the existence of a Test Act, whereby those who might injure that which the State has undertaken to protect are deprived of their power to evil. And, in return, the Church engages to ' apply its utmost endeavours in the service of the State '. It becomes attached to its benefactor from the privilege it receives; and the dangers which might arise from its natural independence are thus obviated. For a federal union precludes the grave problem of an *imperium in imperio,* and the ' mischiefs which so terrified Hobbes ' are met by the terms upon which it is founded.

It is easy enough to discover the loopholes in the theory. The contract does not exist, or, at least, it is placed by Warburton ' in the same archive with the famous original compact between monarch and people ' which has been the object of vast but fruitless searches. Nor does the Act of Submission bear upon its face the marks of that tender care of the protection of an independent society which Warburton declared a vital tenet of the Union. Yet such criticisms miss the real significance of the theory. It is really the introduction into English politics of that notion of the two societies which, a century before, Melville and Bellarmine had made so fruitful. With neither Presbyterian nor Jesuit was the separation complete, for the simple reason that each

F

had a secret conviction that the ecclesiastical society was at bottom the superior. Yet the theory was the parent of liberty, if only because it pointed the way to a balance of power between claims which, before, had seemed mutually exclusive.

Until the Toleration Act, the theory was worthless to the English Church because its temper, under the aegis of Laudian views, had been in substance theocratic. But after 1692 it aptly expressed the compromise the dominant party of the Church had then in mind. They did, indeed, mistake the power of the Church, or, rather, they submitted to the State so fully that what they had intended for a partnership became an absorption. So that the Erastianism of the eighteenth century goes deep enough to make the Church no more than a moral police department of the State. Saints like Ken and preachers like South are replaced by fashionable prelates like Cornwallis, who made Lambeth Palace an adjunct to Ranelagh Gardens, and self-seeking pluralists like Bishop Watson. The Church could not even perceive the meaning of the Wesleyan revolt; and its charity was the irritating and complacent patronage of the obstrusive Hannah More. Its learning decayed, its intelligence slumbered; and the main function it fulfilled until Newman's advent was the provision of rich preferment to the younger sons of the nobility. It is a far cry from Lake of Chichester and Bishop Ken to a Church which was merely an annex to the iniquities of the civil list.

## III

No one can mistake the significance of this conflict. The opponents of Erastianism had a deep sense of their corporate Church, and it was a plea for ecclesiastical freedom that they were making. They saw that a Church whose patronage and discipline and debates were under the control of an alien body could not with honesty claim that Christ was in truth their head. If the Church was to be at the mercy of private judgement and political expediency, the notion of a dogmatic basis would have to be abandoned. Here, indeed, is the root of the condemnation of Tindal and of Hoadly; for they made it, by their teaching, impossible for the Church to possess an ethos of her own. It was thus against the sovereignty of the State that they protested. Somewhere, a line must be drawn about its functions that the independence of the Church might be safeguarded. For its supporters could not be true to their divine mission if the accidental vote of a secular authority was by right to impose its will upon the Church. The view of it as simply a religious body to which the State had conceded certain rights and dignities, they repudiated with passion. The life of the Church was not derived from the State; and for the latter to attempt its circumscription was to usurp an authority not rightly its own.

The real difficulty of this attitude lay in the establishment. For here the Church was, at bottom, declaring that the State life must be lived upon terms of her own definition. That was possible before the Reformation; but with the advent of Nonconformity and the growth of rationalism the exclusive character of the Church's

solution had become unacceptable. If the Church was
to become so intimately involved with the State as an
establishment implied, it had no right to complain if
statesmen with a genius for expediency were willing to
sacrifice it to the attainment of that ideal. For the real
secret of independence is, after all, no more than independence. The Church sought it without being willing
to pay the price. And this it is which enabled Hoadly
to emerge triumphant from an ordeal where logically
he should have failed. The State, by definition, is an
absorptive animal; and the Church had no right to
complain if the price of its privileges was royal supremacy. A century so self-satisfied as the eighteenth would
not have faced the difficulties involved in giving political
expression to the High Church theory.

Yet the protest remained, and it bore a noble fruit
in the next century. The Oxford Movement is usually
regarded as a return to the seventeenth century, to the
ideals, that is to say, of Laud and Andrews.[1] In fact,
its real kinship is with Atterbury and Law. Like them,
it was searching the secret of ecclesiastical independence,
and like them it discovered that connexion with the
State means, in the end, the sacrifice of the Church to
the needs of each political situation. ' The State has
deserted us ', wrote Newman; and the words might
have been written of the earlier time. The Oxford Movement, indeed, like its predecessor, built upon foundations
of sand; and when Lord Brougham told the House of
Lords that the idea of the Church possessing ' absolute
and unalienable rights ' was a ' gross and monstrous
anomaly ' because it would make impossible the supremacy of Parliament, he simply announced the result of

[1] Cf. my *Problem of Sovereignty*, Chapter III.

a doctrine which, implicit in the Act of Submission, was first completely defined by Wake and Hoadly. Nor has the history of this controversy ended. ' Thoughtful men ', the Archbishop of Canterbury has told the House of Lords,[1] '. . . see the absolute need, if a Church is to be strong and vigorous, for the Church, *qua* church, to be able to say what it can do as a church.' ' The rule of the sovereign, the rule of Parliament,' replied Lord Haldane,[2] ' extend as far as the rule of the Church. They are not to be distinguished or differentiated, and that was the condition under which ecclesiastical power was transmitted to the Church of England.' To-day, that is to say, as in the past, antithetic theories of the nature of the State hinge, in essence, upon the problem of its sovereignty. ' A free Church in a free State ' now, as then, may be our ideal; but we still seek the means wherewith to build it.

[1] *Parliamentary Debates*. Fifth Series, Vol. 34, p. 992 (3 June 1919).
[2] *Parliamentary Debates*. Fifth Series, Vol. 34, p. 1002. The quotation does not fully represent Lord Haldane's views.

## CHAPTER IV

# THE ERA OF STAGNATION

## I

WITH the accession of George I, there ensued an era of unexampled calm in English politics, which lasted until the expulsion of Walpole from power in 1742. No vital questions were debated, nor did problems of principle force themselves into view; and if the Jacobites remained in the background as an element invincibly hostile to absorption, the failure of their effort in 1715 showed how feeble was their hold on English opinion. Not, indeed, that the new dynasty was popular. It had nothing of that romantic glamour of a lost cause so imperishably recorded in Scott's pages. The first Georges were heavy and foreign and meagre-souled; but at least they were Protestant, and, until the reign of George III, they were amenable to management. In the result, an opposition in the classic sense was hardly needed; for the only question to be considered was the personalities who were to share in power. The dominating temper of Walpole decided that issue; and he gave thereby to the political struggle the outlines in which it was encased for a generation.

It is a dull period, but complacent; for it was not an unprosperous time. Agriculture and commerce both were abundant; and the increasing development of towns shows us that the Industrial Revolution loomed

in the near distance. The eager continuance of the
deistic controversy suggests that there was something
of novelty beneath the calm; for Tindal and Woolston
and Chubb struck at the root of religious belief, and
Shaftesbury's exaltation of Hellenism not only contributed to the *Aufklärung* in Scotland, but suggested that
Christian ideals were not to go unchallenged. But the
literature of the time is summarized in Pope; and the
easy neatness of his verses is quaintly representative of
the Georgian peace. Defoe and Swift had both done
their work; and the latter had withdrawn to Ireland
to die like a rat in a hole. Bishop Berkeley, indeed, was
convinced of the decadence of England; but his *Essay
towards Preventing the Ruin of Great Britain* (1721) shows
rather the effect of the speculative mania which cul-
minated in the South Sea Bubble upon a noble moral
nature than a genius for political thought. Certainly no
one in that generation was likely to regard with serious-
ness proposals for the endowment of motherhood and a
tax upon the estate of bachelors. The cynical sophistries
of Mandeville were, despite the indignation they aroused,
more suited to the age that Walpole governed. It is, in
fact, the character of the minister which sets the keynote
of the time. An able speaker, without being a great
orator, a superb administrator, eager rather for power
than for good, rating men low by instinct and corrupting
them by intelligence, Walpole was not the man, either
in type of mind or of temperament, to bring great
questions to the foreground of debate. He was content
to maintain his hold over the respect of the Crown, and
to punish able rivals by exclusion from office. One by
one, the younger men of talent, Carteret, Pulteney,
Chesterfield, Pitt, were driven into hostility. He main-

tained himself in office by a corruption as efficiently administered as it was cynically conceived. An opposition developed less on principle than on the belief that spoils are matter rather for distribution than for concentration. The party so formed had, indeed, little ground save personal animosity upon which to fight; and its ablest exertions could only seize upon a doubtful insult to a braggart sea-captain as the pretext of the war it was Walpole's ambition no less than policy to avoid. From 1726 until 1735 the guiding spirit of the party was Bolingbroke; but in the latter year he quarrelled with Pulteney, nominally its leader, and retired in high dudgeon to France. But in the years of his leadership he had evolved a theory of politics than which nothing so clearly displays the intellectual bankruptcy of the time.

To understand the argument of Bolingbroke it is necessary to remember the peculiar character of his career. He had attained to the highest office under Anne at an exceptionally early age; and his period of power had been distinguished by the vehemence with which he pursued the ideal of a strict division of parties and the expulsion of all alien elements from the government. But he had staked all his fortunes upon a scheme he had neither the resolution to plan nor the courage to execute; and his flight to France, on the Hanoverian accession, had been followed by his proscription. Walpole soon succeeded alike to his reputation and place; and through an enormous bribe to the bottomless pocket of the king's mistress, St. John was enabled to return from exile, though not to political place. His restless mind was dissatisfied with exclusion from power, and he occupied himself with creating an alliance between

the Tories and malcontent Whigs for Walpole's overthrow. The alliance succeeded, though too late for
Bolingbroke to enjoy the fruits of success; but in effecting
the purgation of the Tory party from its taint of
Jacobitism he rendered no inconsiderable service. His
foundation, moreover, of the *Craftsman*—the first official
journal of a political party in England—showed his
appreciation of the technique of political controversy.
Most of it is dead now, and, indeed, no small part of
its contemporary success is due to the making of comment in terms of the immediate situation, as also by its
consistent use of a personal reference which has, save
in the mass, no meaning for to-day. Though, doubtless,
the idea of its inception was derived from journals like
Defoe's *Review* and Leslie's *Rehearsal*, which had won
success, its intimate connexion with the party leadership was a novel element; and it may therein claim a
special relation to the official periodicals of a later
generation.

The reputation of Bolingbroke as a political philosopher is something that our age can hardly understand.
'A solemn trifler', Lord Morley has called him; and it
is difficult to know why his easy declamation was so
long mistaken for profound thought. Much, doubtless,
is due to that personal fascination which made him the
inspiration of men so different as Pope and Voltaire;
and the man who could supply ideas to Chatham and
Disraeli cannot be wholly devoid of merit. Certainly
he wrote well, in that easy elegance of style which was
the delight of the eighteenth century; and he is consistently happy in his choice of adjectives. But his work
is at every point embellished with that affectation of
classical learning which was the curse of his age. He

sought no general truths, and he is free from the accusation of sincerity. Nor has he any enthusiasm save that
of bitter partisanship. He hated Walpole, and his political
writings are, at bottom, no more than an attempt to
generalize his animosity. The *Dissertation on Parties* (1734)
and the *Idea of a Patriot King* (1738) might have betrayed
us, taken alone, into regarding their author as a disinterested observer watching with regret the development of a fatal system; but taken in conjunction with
the *Letter to Sir W. Wyndham* (1717), which was not
published until after his death, and is written with an
acrid cynicism fatal to his claim to honesty, they reveal
the opinions as no more than a mask for ambition born
of hate.

The whole, of course, must have some sort of background; and the *Letters on the Study of History* (1735) was
doubtless intended to supply it. Experience is to be the
test of truth, since history is philosophy teaching by
example. But Bolingbroke's own argument supplies its
refutation. His history is an arbitrary selection of instances intended to illustrate the particular ideas which
happened to be uppermost in his mind. The Roman
consuls were chosen by annual election; whence it is
clear that England should have if not an annual, at
least a triennial parliament. He acknowledges that the
past in some degree unknown determines the present.
He has some not unhappy remarks upon the evils of
an attitude which fails to look upon events from a larger
aspect than their immediate environment. But his
history is intended less to illustrate the working of principle than to collect cases worthy of citation. Time and
space do not exist as categories; he is as content with
a Roman anecdote as with a Stuart illustration. He is

willing, indeed, to look for the causes of the Revolution
as far back as the reign of James I; though he shows
his lack of true perception when he ascribes the true
inwardness of the Reformation to the greed of the
monarch for the spoils of the clergy. At bottom what
mainly impresses him is the immense influence of
personal accident upon events. Intrigue, a sudden dislike, some backstairs piece of gossip, here is the real root
of great changes. And when he expresses a ' thorough
contempt ' for the kind of work scholars such as Scaliger
and Petavius had achieved, he shows his entire ignorance
of the method whereby alone a knowledge of general
principle can be attained.

A clear vision, of course, he has, and he was not
beguiled by high notions of prerogative or the like.
The Divine Right of kings is too stupid to be worth
the trouble of refutation; all that makes a king important
is the authority he exerts. So, too, with the Church; for
Bolingbroke, as a professed Deist, has no trouble with
such matters as the apostolic succession. He makes great
show of his love of liberty, which is the true end of
government; and we are informed with a vast solemnity
of the ' perpetual danger ' in which it always stands.
So that the chief end of patriotism is its maintenance;
though we are never told what liberty is, nor how it is
to be maintained. The social compact seems to win
his approbation and we learn that the secret of the
British constitution is the balance of powers and their
mutual independency. But what the powers are, and
how their independence is preserved we do not learn,
save by an insistence that the safety of Europe is to be
found in playing off the ambitions of France and
Austria against each other; an analogy the rejection of

which has been the secret of English constitutional success. We learn of the evil of standing armies and the danger of septennial Parliaments. We are told that parties are mainly moved by the prospect of enjoying office and vast patronage; and a great enough show is made of his hatred for corruption as to convince at least some critics of distinction of his sincerity. The parties of the time had, as he sees, become divided by no difference save that of interest; and herein, at least, he shows us how completely the principles of the Revolution had become exhausted. He wants severe penalties upon electoral corruption. He would have disfranchised the rotten boroughs and excluded placemen from Parliament. The press was to be free; and there is at least a degree of generous insight in his plea for a wider commercial freedom in colonial matters. Yet what, after all, does this mean save that he is fighting a man with the patronage at his disposal and a majority upon the committee for the settlement of disputed elections? And what else can we see in his desire for liberty of the press save a desire to fight Walpole in the open, without fear of the penalties his former treason had incurred?

His value can be tested in another way. His *Idea of a Patriot King* is the remedy for the ills he has depicted. He was sixty years old when it appeared, and he had then been in active politics for thirty-five years, so that we are entitled to regard it as the fruit of his mature experience. He was too convinced that the constitution was ' in the strictest sense a bargain, a conditional contract between the prince and the people ' to attempt again the erection of a system of prerogative. Yet it is about the person of the monarch that the theory hinges. He is to have no powers inconsistent with the liberties of the people; for such restraints will not shackle his virtues while they limit the evil propensities of a bad king. What is needed is a patriot king who will destroy corruption and awaken the spirit of liberty. His effective government will synchronize with the commencement of his reign; and he will at once dismiss the old and cunning ministers, to replace them by servants who are wise. He will not stand upon party, but upon the State. He will unite the forces of good counsel into a single scheme. Complaints will be answered, the evildoers punished. Commerce will flow on with uninterrupted prosperity, and the navy of England receive its due meed of attention. His conduct must be dignified, and he must acquire his influence not apart from, but on account of, the affection of his people. ' Concord ', says Bolingbroke in rhapsodical prospection, ' will appear breeding peace and prosperity on every hand '; though he prudently hopes also that men will look back with affection upon one ' who desired life for nothing so much as to see a King of Great Britain the most powerful man in the country, and a patriot King at the head of a united people '.

Bolingbroke himself has admitted that such a monarch would be a ' sort of standing miracle ', and perhaps no other comment upon his system is required. A smile in Plato at the sight of his philosopher-king in such strange company might well be pardoned. It is only necessary to point out that the person whom Bolingbroke designates for this high function was Frederick, Prince of Wales, to us the most meagre of a meagre generation, but to Bolingbroke, by whose grace he was captivated, ' the greatest and most glorious of human beings '. This exaltation of the monarch came at a time when a variety of circumstances had combined to show the decrease of monarchical sentiment. It bears upon its every page the marks of a personal antagonism. It is too obviously the programme of a party to be capable of serious interpretation as a system. The minister who is to be impeached, the wise servants who are to gain office, the attack on corruption, the spirited foreign policy—all these have the earmarks of a platform rather than of a philosophy. Attacks on corruption hardly read well in the mouth of a dissolute gambler; and the one solid evidence of deep feeling is the remark on the danger of finance in politics. For none of the Tories save Barnard, who owed his party influence thereto, understood the financial schemes of Walpole; and since they were his schemes obviously they represented the triumph of devilish ingenuity. The return of landed men to power would mean the return of simplicity to politics; and one can imagine the country squires, the last resort of enthusiasm for Church and King, feeling that Bolingbroke had here emphasized the dangers of a régime which already faintly foreshadowed their exclusion from power. The pamphlet was the cornerstone in the education of Frederick's son; and when George III came to the throne he proceeded to give such heed to his master as the circumstances permitted. It is perhaps, as A. L. Smith has argued, unfair to visit Bolingbroke with George's version of his ideal; yet they are sufficiently connected for the one to give the meaning to the other. Chatham, indeed, was later intrigued by this ideal of a national party; and before Disraeli discovered that England does not love coalitions he expended much rhetoric upon the beauties of a patriotic king. But Chatham was a wayward genius who had nothing of

that instinct for common counsel which is of the essence
of party government; while it is necessary to draw a
firm line between Disraeli's genial declamation and his
practice when in office. It is sufficient to say that the
one effort founded upon the principles of Bolingbroke
ended in disaster; and that his own last reflections
express a bitter disillusion at the result of the event
which he looked to as the inauguration of the golden
age.

## II

The fall of Walpole, indeed, released no energies for
political thought; the system continued, though the men
were different. What alone can be detected is the growth
of a democratic opinion which found its sustenance outside the House of Commons, the opinion the strength
of which was later to force the elder Pitt upon an unwilling king. An able pamphlet of the time shows us the
arrival of this unlooked-for portent. *Faction detected by
the Evidence of Facts* (1742) was, though it is anonymous,[1]
obviously written by one in touch with the inner current
of affairs. The author had hoped for the fall of Walpole,
though he sees the chaos in its result. 'A republican
spirit', he says, 'has strangely arisen'; and he goes on
to tell how the electors of London and Westminster were
now regarding their members as delegates to whom instructions might be issued. 'A new party of malcontents'
had arisen, 'assuming to themselves, though very falsely,
the title of the People.' They affect, he tells us, 'superiority to the whole legislature . . . and endeavour in
effect to animate the people to resume into their own

[1] It was probably written by Lord Egmont.

hands that vague and loose authority which exists (unless in theory) in the people of no country upon earth, and the inconvenience of which is so obvious, that it is the first step of mankind, when formed into society, to divest themselves of it, and to delegate it forever from themselves '. The writer clearly foreshadows, even in his dislike, that temper which produced the Wilkes affair, and made it possible for Cartwright and Horne Tooke and Sir Thomas Hollis to become the founders of English radicalism.

Yet the influence of that temper still lay a generation ahead; and the next piece of import comes from a mind which, though perhaps the most powerful of all which have applied themselves to political philosophy in England, was, from its very scepticism, incapable of constructive effort. David Hume was thirty-one years of age when he published (1742) the first series of his essays; and his *Treatise of Human Nature* which had fallen ' dead-born from the press ' was in some sort compensated by the success of the new work. The second part, entitled *Political Discourses*, was published in 1752, almost simultaneously with the *Inquiry concerning the Principles of Morals*. As in the case of Hume's metaphysical studies, they constitute the most powerful dissolvent the century was to see. Yet nowhere was so clearly to be demonstrated the euthanasia into which English politics had fallen.

Hume, of course, is always critical and suggestive, and even if he had no distinctive contribution to make, he gave a new turn to speculation. There is something almost of magic in the ease with which he demolishes Divine Right and the social contract. The one is an inevitable deduction from theism, but it protects a usurper not less than an hereditary king, and gives a 'divine commission' as well to a constable as to the most majestic prince. The proponents of the social contract are in no better case. ' Were you to preach ', he remarks, ' in most parts of the world that political connexions are founded altogether on voluntary consent, or on a mutual promise, the magistrate would soon imprison you as seditious for loosening the ties of obedience; if your friends did not before shut you up as delirious for advancing such absurdities.' The original contract could not be produced, and, even if it were, it would suppose the ' consent of the fathers to bind the children even to the most remote generations '. The real truth, as he remarks, is that ' almost all the governments which exist at present, or of which there remains any record in story, have been founded originally on usurpation, or on conquest, or both, without any pretence of a fair consent or voluntary subjection of the people '. If we then ask why obedience is possible, the sufficient answer is that ' it becomes so familiar that most men never make any inquiry about its origin or cause, any more than about the principle of gravity, resistance, or the most universal laws of nature '.

Government, in short, is dependent upon the inescapable facts of psychology. It might be unnecessary if all desires could be individually fulfilled by making them, or if man showed to his fellow-men the same tender regard he has for himself. So happy a condition does not exist; and government is the most useful way of remedying the defects of our situation. A theologian might say that Hume derives government from original sin; to which he would have replied by denying the fall. His whole attitude is simply an insistence that

G

utility is the touchstone of institutions, and he may claim to be the first thinker who attempted its application to the whole field of political science. He knows that opinion is the sovereign ruler of mankind, and that ideas of utility lie at the base of the thoughts which get accepted. He does not, indeed, deny that fear and consent enter into the attitude of men; he simply asserts that these also are founded upon a judgement of utility in the thing judged. We obey because otherwise ' society could not subsist ', and society subsists for its utility. ' Men ', he says, ' could not live at all in society, at least in civilized society, without laws and magistrates and judges, to prevent the encroachments of the strong upon the weak, of the violent upon the just and equitable.'

Utilitarianism is, of course, above all a method; and it is not unfair to say of Hume that he did not get very far beyond insistence on that point. He sees that the subjection of the many to the few is rooted in human impulse; but he has no penetrating inquiry, such as that of Locke or Hobbes, into the purpose of such subjection. So, too, it is the sense of public interest which determines men's thoughts on government, on who should rule, and what should be the system of property; but the ethical substance of these questions he leaves undetermined. Politics, he thinks, may one day be a science; though he considers the world still too young for general truths therein. The maxims he suggests as of permanent value, ' that a hereditary prince, a nobility without vassals, and a people voting by their representatives form the best monarchy, autocracy and democracy '; that ' free governments . . . are the most ruinous and oppressive to their provinces '; that republics are more favourable to science, monarchies to art; that the

death of a political body is inevitable; would none of
them, probably, be accepted by most thinkers at the
present time. And when he constructs an ideal constitution, irrespective of time and place, which is to be
regarded as practical because it resembles that of Holland, it is obvious that the historical method had not
yet come fully into being.

Yet Hume is full of flashes of deep wisdom, and it
would be an avoidance of justice not to note the extent
of the spasmodic insight that he had. He has a keen eye
for the absurdity of Pope's maxim that administration
is all in all; nothing can ever make the forms of government immaterial. He accepts Harrington's dictum that
the substance of government corresponds to the distribution of property, without making it, as later thinkers
have done, the foundation of all political forces. He sees
that the Crown cannot influence the mass of men, or
withstand the new balance of property in the State; a
prophecy of which the accuracy was demonstrated by
the failure of George III. 'In all governments', as he says,
' there is a perpetual intestinal struggle, open or secret ',
between Authority and Liberty; though his judgement
that neither ' can ever absolutely prevail ', shows us
rather that we are on the threshold of *laissez-faire* than
that Hume really understood the problem of freedom.
He realized that the House of Commons had become
the pivot of State; though he looked with dread upon
the onset of popular government. He saw the inevita-
bility of parties, as also their tendency to persist in
terms of men instead of principles. He was convinced
of the necessity of liberty to the progress of the arts and
sciences; and no one, save Adam Smith, has more
acutely insisted upon the evil effect on commerce of an

absolute government. He emphasized the value of freedom of the press, in which he saw the secret whereby
the mixed government of England was maintained. ' It
has also been found ', he said in a happy phrase, '. . . that
the people are no such dangerous monsters as they have
been represented, and that it is in every respect better
to guide them like rational creatures than to lead or
drive them like brute beasts.' There is, in fact, hardly
a page of his work in which some such acuteness may not
be found.

Not, indeed, that a curious blindness is absent. Hume
was a typical child of one aspect of the eighteenth century in his hatred of enthusiasm, and the form in which
he most abominates it is religious. Why people's religious
opinions should lead to antagonism he could no more
understand than why people should refuse to pass one
another on a road. Wars of religion thus seemed to
him based upon a merely frivolous principle; and in
his ideal commonwealth he made the Church a department of the State lest it should get out of hand. He was,
moreover, a static philosopher, disturbed by signs of
political restlessness; and this led to the purgation of
Whig doctrines from his writings, and their consistent
replacement by a cynical conservatism. He was always
afraid that popular government would mean mob-rule;
and absolute government is accordingly recommended
as the euthanasia of the British constitution. Not even
the example of Sweden convinced him that a standing
army might exist without civil liberty being endangered;
and he has all the noxious fallacies of his time upon the
balance of power. Above all, it is striking to see his
helplessness before the problem of national character.
Mainly he ascribes it to the form of government, and

that in turn to chance. Even the friend of Montesquieu can see no significance in race or climate. The idea, in fact, of evolution is entirely absent from his political speculation. Political life, like human life, ends in death; and the problem is to make our egress as comfortable as we can, for the prime evil is disturbance. It is difficult not to feel that there is almost a physical basis in his own disease for this love of quiet. The man who put indolence among the primary motives of human happiness was not likely to view novel theories with unruffled temper.

Hume has an eminent place among economists, and for one to whom the study of such phenomena was but a casual inquiry, it is marvellous how much he saw. He is free from the crude errors of mercantilism; and, twenty years before Adam Smith, hopes, 'as a British subject', for the prosperity of other countries. 'Free communication and exchange' seems to him an ordinance of nature; and he heaps contempt upon those 'numberless bars, obstructions and imposts which all nations of Europe, and none more than England, have put upon trade'. Specie he places in its true light as merely a medium of exchange. The supposed antagonism between commerce and agriculture he disposes of in a half-dozen effective sentences. He sees the place of time and distance in the discussion of economic want. He sees the value of a general level of economic equality, even while he is sceptical of its attainment. He insists upon the economic value of high wages, though he somewhat belittles the importance of wealth in the achievement of happiness. Before Bentham, who on this point converted Adam Smith, he knew that the rate of interest depends upon the supply of and demand for loans. He insists that commerce demands a free government for its progress, pointing out, doubtless from his abundant French experience, that an absolute government gives to the commercial class an insufficient status of honour. He pointed out, doubtless with France again in his mind, the evils of an arbitrary system of taxation. ' They are commonly converted ', he says with unwonted severity, ' into punishments on industry; and also, by their unavoidable inequality, are more grievous, than by the real burden which they impose.' And he emphasizes his belief that the best taxes are those which, like taxes upon luxury, press least upon the poor.

Such insight is extraordinary enough in the pre-Adamite epoch; but even more remarkable are his psychological foundations. The wealth of the State, he says, is the labour of its subjects, and they work because the wants of man are not a stated sum, but ' multiply every moment upon him '. The desire for wealth comes from the idea of pleasure; and in the *Treatise on Human Nature* he discusses with superb clarity the way in which the idea of pleasure is related at once to individual satisfaction and to that sympathy for others which is one of the roots of social existence. He points out the need for happiness in work. ' The mind ', he writes, ' acquires new vigour, enlarges its powers and faculties, and by an assiduity in honest industry both satisfies its own appetites and prevents growth of unnatural ones '; though, like his predecessor, Francis Hutcheson, he over-emphasizes the delights opened by civilization to the humbler class of men. He gives large space in his discussion to the power of will; and, indeed, one of the main advantages he ascribed to government was the compulsion it puts upon us to allow the categories of time and space a part in our calculations. He does not, being in his own life entirely free from avarice, regard the appetite for riches as man's main motive to existence; though no one was more urgent in his insistence that ' the avidity of acquiring goods and possessions for ourselves and our nearest friends is . . . destructive of society' unless balanced by considerations of justice. And what he therein intended may be gathered from the liberal notions of equality he manifested. ' Every person ', he wrote in a famous passage, ' if possible ought to enjoy the fruits of his labour in a full possession of all the necessaries, and many of the conveniences of life. No one can doubt but such an equality is most suitable to human nature, and diminishes much less the happiness of the rich than it adds to that of the poor.' It is clear that we have moved far from the narrow confines of the old political arithmetic. The theory of utility enables Hume to see the scope of economics— the word itself he did not know—in a more generous perspective than at any previous time. It would be too much to say that his grasp of its psychological foundation enabled him entirely to move from the limitations of the older concept of a national prosperity expressed only in terms of bullion to the view of economics as a social science. But at least he saw that economics is rooted in the nature of men and therein he had the secret of its true understanding. *The Wealth of Nations* would less easily have made its way had not the insight of Hume prepared the road for its reception.

What, then, and in general, is his place in the history of political thought? Clearly enough, he is not the founder of a system; his work is rather a series of pregnant hints than a consecutive account of political facts. Nor must we belittle the debt he owes to his predecessors. Much, certainly, he owed to Locke, and the full radiance of the Scottish enlightenment emerges into the day with his teaching. Francis Hutcheson gave him no small inspiration; and Hutcheson means that he was indebted to Shaftesbury. Indeed, there is much of the sturdy common sense of the Scottish school about him, particularly perhaps in that interweaving of ethics, politics, and economics, which is characteristic of the school from Hutcheson in the middle seventeenth century, to the able, if neglected, Lorimer in the nineteenth.[1] He is entitled to be considered the real founder of utilitarianism. He first showed how difficult it is in politics to draw a distinction between ethical right and men's opinion of what ought to be. He brings to an end what Coleridge happily called the ' metapolitical school '. After him we are done with the abuse of history to bolster up Divine Right and social contract; for there is clearly present in his use of facts a true sense of historical method. He put an end also to the confusion which resulted from the effort of thinkers to erect standards of right and wrong independent of all positive law. He took the facts as phenomena to be explained rather than as illustrations of some favourite thesis to be maintained in part defiance of them. Conventional Whiggism has no foothold after he has done with its analysis. His utilitarianism was the first efficient substitute for the laboured metaphysics of the contract school; and even if he was not the first to see through its pretensions— that is perhaps the claim of Shaftesbury—he was the

[1] There are few books which show so clearly as Lorimer's *Institutes of Nations* (1872) how fully the Scottish school was in the midstream of European thought.

first to show the grounds of their uselessness. He saw that history and psychology together provide the materials for a political philosophy. So that even if he could not himself construct it, the hints at least were there.

His suggestiveness, indeed, may be measured in another fashion. The metaphysics of Burke, so far as one may use a term he would himself have repudiated, are largely those of Hume. The place of habit and of social instinct alongside of consent, the perception that reason alone will not explain political facts, the emphasis upon resistance as of last resort, the denial that allegiance is a mere contract to be presently explained, the deep respect for order—all these are, after all, the fabric from which the thought of Burke was woven. Nor is there in Bentham's defence of utilitarianism, argument in which he would have recognized novelty. Herein, at least, his proof that morality is no more than general opinion of utility constructs, in briefer form, the later arguments of Bentham, Paley, and the Mills; nor can their mode of statement claim superiority to Hume's. So that on either side of his work he foreshadows the advent of the two great schools of modern political thought. His utilitarianism is the real path by which radical opinion at last found means of acceptance. His use of history is, through Burke, the ancestor of that specialized conservatism begotten of the historical method. If there is thus so much, it is, of course, tempting to ask why there is not more. If Hume has the materials why did he fail to build up a system from them? The answer seems twofold. In part it is the man himself. His genius, as his metaphysics show, lay essentially in his power of destruction; and the man who gave solipsism to philosophy was not likely to effect a new creation in politics. In part, also, the condition of the time gave little stimulus to novelty. Herein Hume was born a generation too early. Had he written when George III attempted the destruction of the system of the Revolution, and when America and France combined to raise again the basic questions of politics, he might have done therein what Adam Smith effected in his own field. But the time had not yet come; and it was left to Burke and Bentham to reap where he had sown.

## CHAPTER V

# SIGNS OF CHANGE

## I

FROM Hume until the publication of Burke's *Present Discontents* (1770) there is no work on English politics of the first importance. Walpole had fallen in 1742; but for the next fifteen years his methods dominated the parliamentary scene. It was only with the advent of the elder Pitt to power that a new temper may be observed, a temper quickened by what followed on the accession of George III. Henceforward, it is not untrue to say that the early complacency of the time was lost; or, at least, it was no longer in the ascendant again until the excesses of the French Revolution enabled Burke to persuade his countrymen into that grim satisfaction with their own achievement of which Lord Eldon is the standing model. The signs of change are in each instance slight, though collectively they acquire significance. It was difficult for men to grumble where, as under Walpole, each harvest brought them greater prosperity, or where, as under Chatham, they leaped from victory to victory. Something of the exhilaration of these years we can still catch in the letters which show the effort made by the jaded Horace Walpole to turn off with easy laughter his deep sense of pride. In the House of Commons, indeed, there is nothing, until the Wilkes case, to show that a new age has come. It is the novels of Richardson and Fielding, the first shy hints of the romantic temper in Gray and Collins, above all in the awakening of political science, that novelty is apparent.

So far as a new current of thought can ever be referred to a single source, the French influence is the effective cause of change. Voltaire and Montesquieu had both visited England in the period of Walpole's administration, and both had been greatly influenced by what they saw. Rousseau, indeed, came later on that amazing voyage which the good-natured Hume insisted would save him from his dread of persecution, and there is evidence enough that he did not relish his experience. Yet when he came, in 1762, to publish the *Contrat Social* it was obvious that he had drunk deeply of English thought. The real meaning of their work to Englishmen lay in the perspective they gave to English institutions. Naturally enough, there was a vast difference between the simplicity of a government where sovereignty was the monarch's will and one in which a complex distribution of powers was found to secure a general freedom. The Frenchmen were amazed at the generous equality of English judicial procedure. The liberty of unlicensed printing—less admirable than they accounted it—the difference between a *Habeas Corpus* and a *lettre de cachet*, the regular succession of Parliaments, all these impressed them, who knew the meaning of their absence, as a magnificent achievement. The English constitution revealed to France an immense and unused reservoir of philosophic illustration. Even to England itself that meaning was but partly known. Locke's system was a generalization from its significance at a special crisis. Hume had partial glimpses of its inner substance. But for most it had become a discreet series of remedies for particular wrongs. Its analysis as a connected whole invigorated thought as nothing had done since the Civil Wars had elaborated the theory of parliamentary sovereignty. What was more significant was the realization of Montesquieu's import simultaneously with the effort of George III to revive crown influence. Montesquieu thus became the prophet of a new race of thinkers. Rousseau's time was not yet; though within a score of years it was possible to see him as the rival to Burke's conservatism.

It is worth while to linger for a moment upon the thesis which underlies the *Esprit des Lois* (1748). It is a commonplace now that Montesquieu is to be regarded as the founder of the historical method. The present is to be explained by its ancestry. Laws, governments, customs are not truths absolute and universal, but relative to the time of their origin and the country from which they derive. It would be inaccurate, with Rousseau on the threshold, to say that his influence demolished the systems of political abstraction which, at their logical best, and in the most complete unreality, are to be found in Godwin's *Political Justice*; but it is not beyond the mark to affirm that after his time such asbtract systems were on the defensive. Therein, with all his faults, he had given Burke the clue to those truths he so profoundly saw—the sense of the State as more than a mechanical contrivance, the high regard for prescription, the sense of law as the voice of past wisdom. He was, said Burke, ' the greatest genius which has enlightened this age '; and Burke had every reason to utter that noble panegyric. But Montesquieu was more than this. He emphasized legislation as the main mechanism of social change; and therein he is the parent of that decisive reversal of past methods of which Bentham first revealed the true significance. Nor had any thinker before his time so emphasized the importance of liberty as the true end of government; even the placid Blackstone adopted the utterance from him in his inaugural lecture as Vinerian professor. He insisted, too, on the danger of perversion to which political principle lies open; a feeling which found consistent utterance both in the debates of the Philadelphia Convention and in the writings of Bentham and James Mill. What, perhaps, is most immediately significant is his famous praise of the British constitution—the secret of which he entirely misapprehended—and his discovery of its essence in the separation of powers. The short sixth chapter of his eleventh book is the real keynote of Blackstone and De Lolme. It led them to investigate, on principles of at least doubtful validity, an edifice never before described in detail. It is, when the last criticism has been made, an immense step forward from the uncouth antiquarianism of Coke's Second Institute to the neatly reticulated structure erected upon the foundations of Montesquieu's hint. That it was wrong was less important than that the attempt should have been made. The evil that men do lives after them; and few doctrines have been more noxious in their consequence than this theory of checks and balances. But Blackstone's *Commentaries* (1765-9) produced Bentham's *Fragment on Government* (1776), and with that book we enter upon the realistic study of the British constitution.

Rousseau is in an antithetic tradition; but just as he drew from English thinkers so did he exercise upon the next generation an influence the more logical because the inferences he drew were those that his masters, with the English love of compromise, had sought to avoid. Rousseau is the disciple of Locke; and the real difference between them is no more than a removal of the limitations upon the power of government which Locke had proposed. It is a removal at every point conditioned by the interest of the people. For Rousseau declared that the existing distribution of power in Europe was a monstrous thing, and he made the people sovereign that there might be no hindrance to their achievement in the shape of sinister interest. The powers of the people thus became their rights and herein was an unlimited sanction for innovation. It is easy enough then to understand why such a philosophy should have been anathema to Burke. Rousseau's eager sympathy for humble men, his optimistic faith in the immediate prospect of popular power were to Burke the symptoms of insane delusion and their author ' the great professor and founder of the philosophy of vanity in England '. But Burke forgot that the real secret of Rousseau's influence was the success of the American Revolution; and no one had done more than Burke himself to promote its cause and justify its principles. That revolution established what Europe might well consider a democracy; and its statesmen were astonished not less at the vigilance with which America guarded against the growth of autocratic government, than at the soberness with which it checked the supposed weakness of the sovereign people. America made herself independent while what was best in Europe combined in enthusiastic applause; and it seemed as though the maxims of Rousseau had been taken to heart and that a single, vigorous exertion of power could remove what deliberation was impotent to secure. Here Rousseau had a message for Great Britain which Burke at every stage denied. Nor, at the moment, was it influential except in the general impetus it gave to thought. But from the moment of its appearance it is an undercurrent of decisive importance; and while in its metaphysical form it failed to command acceptance, in the hands of Bentham its results were victorious. Bentham differs from Rousseau not in the conclusions he recommends so much as in the language in which he clothes them. Either make a final end of the optimism of men like Hume and Blackstone, or the veneration for the past which is at the root of Burke's own teaching.

It is easy to see why thought such as this should have given the stimulus it did. Montesquieu came to praise the British constitution at a time when good men were aghast at its perversion. There was no room in many years for revolution, but at least there was place for hearty discontent and a seeking after new methods. Of that temper two men so different as the elder Pitt and Wilkes are the political symbols. The former's rise to power upon the floodtide of popular enthusiasm meant nothing so much as a protest against the cynical corruption of the previous generation. Wilkes was a sign that the populace was slowly awaking to a sense of its own power. The French creed was too purely logical, too obviously the outcome of alien conditions, to fit in its entirety the English facts; and, it must be admitted, memories of wooden shoes played not a little part in its rejection. The rights of man made only a partial appeal until the miseries of Pitt's wars showed what was involved in that rejection; and then it was too late. But no one could feel without being stirred the illumination of Montesquieu; and Rousseau's questions, even if they proved unanswerable, were stuff for thought. The work of the forty years before the French Revolution is nothing so much as a preparation for Bentham. The torpor slowly passes. The theorists build an edifice each part of which a man whose passion is attuned to the English nature can show to be obsolete and ugly. If the French thinkers had conferred no other benefit, that, at least, would have been a supreme achievement.

## II

The first book to show the signs of change came in 1757. John Brown's *Estimate of the Manners and Principles of the Times* is largely forgotten now; though it went through seven editions in a year and was at once translated into French. Brown was a clergyman, a minor planet in the vast Warburtonian system, who had already published a volume of comment upon the *Characteristics* of Shaftesbury. His book is too evidently modelled upon Montesquieu, whom he mentions with reverence, to make us doubt its derivation. There is the same reliance upon Livy and Machiavelli, the same attempt at striking generalization; though the argument upon which Brown's conclusions are based is seldom given, perhaps because his geometric clarity of statement impressed him as self-demonstrative. Brown's volumes are an essay upon the depravity of the times. He does not deny it humanitarianism, and a still lingering sense of freedom, but it is steeped in corruption and displays nothing so much as a luxurious and selfish effeminacy. He condemns the universities out of hand, in phrases which Gibbon and Adam Smith would not have rejected. He deplores the decay of taste and learning. Men trifle with Hume's

H

gay impieties, and could not, if they would, appreciate
the great works of Bishop Warburton. Politics has become nothing save a means of promoting selfish interests.
The church, the theatre, and the arts have all of them
lost their former virtues. The neurotic temper of the
times is known to all. The nation, as was shown in 1745,
when a handful of Highlanders penetrated without
opposition to the heart of the kingdom, has grown slack
and cowardly. Gambling penetrates every nook and
cranny of the upper class; the officers of the army devote
themselves to fashion; the navy's main desire is for
prize money. Even the domestic affections are at a low
ebb; and the grand tour brings back a new species of
Italianate Englishman. The poor, indeed, the middle
class, and the legal and medical professions, Brown
specifically exempts from this indictment. But he emphasizes his belief that this is unimportant. ' The manners
and principles of those who lead ', he says, '. . . not of
those who are governed . . . will ever determine the
strength or weakness, and therefore, the continuance or
dissolution of a state.'

This profligacy Brown compares to the languid vice
which preceded the fall of Carthage and of Rome; and
he sees the approaching ruin of Great Britain at the
hands of France, unless it can be cured. So far as he
has an explanation to offer, it seems to be the fault of
Walpole, and the decay of religious sentiment. His
remedy is only Bolingbroke's Patriot King, dressed up
in the habit of the elder Pitt, now risen to the height of
power. What mainly stirred Englishmen was the prophecy of defeat on the morrow of the disastrous convention of Kloster Seven; but when Wolfe and Clive re-
paired that royal humiliation Brown seems to have died

a natural death. What is more interesting than his prophecies was the evidence of a close reading of Montesquieu. English liberty, he says, is the product of the climate; a kind of mixture, it appears, of fog and sullen temper. Nations inevitably decay, and the commercial grandeur of England is the symptom of old age; it means a final departure from the simplicity of nature and breeds the luxury which kills by enervation. Brown has no passion, and his book reads rather like Galsworthy's *Island Pharisees* sufficiently expurgated to be declaimed by a well-bred clergyman in search of preferment on the ground of attention to the evils of his time. It describes undoubted facts, and it shows that the era of content has gone. But its careful periods and strangely far-off air lack the eagerness for truth which Rousseau put into his questions. Brown can neither explain nor can he proffer remedy. He sees that Pitt is somehow significant; but when he rules out the popular voice as devoid of all importance, he deprives himself of the means whereby to grasp the meaning of the power that Pitt exerted. Nothing could prove more strongly the exactitude of Burke's *Present Discontents*. Nothing could better justify the savage indignation of Junius.

Hume was the friend of Montesquieu, though twenty years his junior; and the *Esprit des Lois* travelled rapidly to Scotland. There it caught the eye of Adam Ferguson, the author of a treatise on refinement, and, by the influence of Hume and Adam Smith, Professor of Moral Philosophy in the University of Edinburgh. Ferguson seems to have been immensely popular in his time, and certainly he has a skill for polished phrase and a genial paraphrase of other men's ideas. His *Essay on the History of Civil Society* (1767), which in a quarter of a century went through six editions, was thought by Helvétius superior to Montesquieu, though Hume himself, as always the incarnation of kindness, recommended its suppression. At least Ferguson read enough of Montesquieu to make some fluent generalities sound plausible. He knows that the investigation of savage life will throw some light upon the origins of government. He sees the folly of generalizing easily upon the state of nature. He insists, probably after conversation with Adam Smith, upon the social value of the division of functions. He does not doubt the original equality of men. He thinks the luxury of his age has reached the limit of its useful growth. Property he traces back to a parental desire to make a better provision for children ' than is found under the promiscuous management of many co-partners '. Climate has the new importance upon which Montesquieu has insisted; or, at least, as it ' ripens the pineapple and the tamarina ', so it ' inspires a degree of mildness that can even assuage the rigours of despotical government '. The priesthood—this is Hume—becomes a separate influence under the sway of superstition. Liberty, he says, ' is maintained by the continued differences and opposition of numbers, not by their concurring zeal in behalf of equitable government '. The hand that can bend Ulysses' bow is certainly not here; and this pinchbeck Montesquieu can best be left in the obscurity into which he has fallen. The *Esprit des Lois* took twenty years in writing; and it needed the immense researches of men like Savigny before its significance could fully be grasped. Facile popularizers of this sort may have mollified the drawing-room; but they did not add to political ideas.

## III

A more fertile source of inquiry was to be found among the students of constitutional law. Blackstone's *Commentaries on the Laws of England* (1765–9) has had ever since its first publication an authority such as Coke only before possessed. ' He it is ', said Bentham, ' who, first of all institutional writers, has taught jurisprudence to speak the language of the Scholar and the Gentleman.' Certainly, as Professor Dicey has remarked, ' the book contains much real learning about our system of government '. We are less concerned here with Blackstone as an antiquarian lawyer than as a student of political philosophy. Here his purpose seems obvious enough. The English constitution raised him from humble means through a professorship at Oxford to a judgeship in the Court of Common Pleas. He had been a member of Parliament and refused the office of Solicitor-General. He had thus no reason to be dissatisfied with the conditions of his time; and the first book of the *Commentaries* is nothing so much as an attempt to explain why English constitutional law is a miracle of wisdom.

Constitutional law, as such, indeed, found no place in Blackstone's book. It creeps in under the rights of persons, where he deals with the power of King and Parliament. His treatment implies a whole philosophy. Laws are of three kinds—of Nature, of God, and of the civil State. Civil law, with which alone he is concerned, is ' a rule of civil conduct prescribed by the supreme power in a state, commanding what is right and prohibiting what is wrong '. It is, he tells us, ' called a rule to distinguish it from a compact or agreement '. It

derives from the sovereign power, of which the chief
character is the making of laws. Society is based upon
the ' wants and fears ' of men; and it is coeval with their
origin. The idea of a state of nature ' is too wild to be
seriously admitted ', besides being contrary to historical
knowledge. Society implies government, and whatever
its origins or its forms there ' must be in all of them a
supreme, irresistible, absolute, uncontrolled authority,
in which the *jura summa imperii*, or rights of sovereignty
reside '. The forms of government are classified in the
usual way; and the British constitution is noted as a
happy mixture of them all. ' The legislature of the Kingdom ', Blackstone writes, ' is entrusted to three powers
entirely independent of each other; first the King,
secondly the lords spiritual and temporal, which is an
aristocratical assembly of persons, chosen for their piety,
their birth, their wisdom, their valour or their property;
and, thirdly, the House of Commons, freely chosen by
the people from among themselves, which makes it a
kind of democracy; and as this aggregate body, actuated
by different springs and attentive to different interests,
composes the British Parliament and has the supreme
disposal of everything; there can be no inconvenience
attempted by either of the three branches, but will be
withstood by one of the other two; each branch being
armed with a negative power, sufficient to repel any
innovation which it shall think inexpedient or dangerous.' It is in the king in Parliament that British
sovereignty resides. Eschewing the notion of an original
contract, Blackstone yet thinks that all the implications
of it are secured. ' The constitutional government of this
island ', he says, ' is so admirably tempered and compounded, that nothing can endanger or hurt it, but

destroying the equilibrium of power between one branch of the legislature and the rest.'

All this is not enough; though, as Bentham was to show in his *Fragment on Government*, it is already far too much. ' A body of nobility ', such is the philosophic interpretation of the House of Lords, ' is also more peculiarly necessary in our mixed and compounded constitution, in order to support the rights of both the Crown and People, by forming a barrier to withstand the encroachments of both . . . if they were confounded with the mass of the people, and like them had only a vote in electing representatives, their privileges would soon be borne down and overwhelmed by the popular torrent, which would effectually level all distinctions.' ' The Commons ', he says further, ' consist of all such men of property in the kingdom as have not seats in the House of Lords.' The legal irresponsibility of the king is emphasized. ' He is not only incapable of doing wrong,' says Blackstone, ' but even of thinking wrong; he can never mean to do an improper thing; in him is no folly or weakness ', though he points out that the constitution ' has allowed a latitude of supposing the contrary '. The powers of the king are described in terms more suitable to the iron despotism of William the Norman than to the backstairs corruption of George III. The right of revolution is noted, with justice, as belonging to the sphere of morals rather than of law.

' Its true defect ', says Professor Dicey of the *Commentaries*, ' is the hopeless confusion both of language and of thought introduced into the whole subject of constitutional law by Blackstone's habit—common to all the lawyers of his time—of applying old and inapplicable terms to new institutions.' This is severe enough; yet

Blackstone's 'sins are deeper than the criticism would suggest. He introduced into English political philosophy that systematic attention to forms instead of substance upon which the whole vicious theory of checks and balances was erected. He made no distinction between the unlimited sovereignty of law and the very obviously limited sovereignty of reality. He must have known that to talk of the independence of the branches of the legislature was simple nonsense at a time when king and peers competed for the control of elections to the House of Commons. His idealization of a peerage whose typical spiritual member was Archbishop Cornwallis and whose temporal embodiment was the Duke of Bedford would not have deceived a schoolboy had it not provided a bulwark against improvement. It was ridiculous to describe the Commons as representative of property so long as places like Manchester and Sheffield were virtually disfranchised. His picture of the royal prerogative was a portrait against every detail of which what was best in England had struggled in the preceding century and a half. He has nothing to say of the Cabinet, nothing of ministerial responsibility, nothing of the party-system. What he did was to produce the defence of a non-existent system which acted as a barrier to all legal, and much political, progress in the next half-century. He gave men material without cause for satisfaction.

As a description of the existing government there is thus hardly an element of Blackstone's work which could stand the test of critical inquiry. But even worse was its philosophy. As Bentham pointed out, he was unaware of the distinction between society and government. The state of nature exists, or fails to exist, with startling inconsistency. Blackstone, in fact, was a Lockian who knows that Hume and Montesquieu have cut the ground from under his master's feet, and yet cannot understand how, without him, a foundation is to be supplied. Locke, indeed, seems to him, as a natural conservative, to go too far, and he rejects the original contract as without basis in history; yet contractual notions are present at every fundamental stage of his argument. The sovereign power, so we are told, is irresistible; and then because Blackstone is uncertain what right is to mean, we hear of moral limitations upon its exercise. He speaks continually of representation without any effort to examine into the notions it conveys. The members of society are held to be equal; and great pains are taken to justify existent inequalities. ' The natural foundations of sovereignty ', he writes, ' are the three great requisites . . . of wisdom, goodness and power.' Yet there is nowhere any proof in his book that steps have been taken in the British constitution to associate these with the actual exertion of authority. Nor has he clear notions of the way in which property is to be founded. Communism, he writes in seventeenth-century fashion, is the institution of the all-beneficent Creator who gave the earth to men; property comes when men occupy some special portion of the soil continuously or mix their labour with movable possessions. This is pure Locke; though the conclusions drawn by Blackstone are utterly remote from the logical result of his own premisses.

The truth surely is that Blackstone had, upon all these questions, only the most confused sort of notions. He had to preface his work with some sort of philosophic theory because the conditions of the age demanded it. The one source of enlightenment when he wrote was Hume; but for some uncertain reason, perhaps his piety,

Blackstone makes no reference to the great sceptic's speculations. So that he was driven back upon notions he felt to be false, without a proper realization of their falsity. His use of Montesquieu shows rather how dangerous a weapon a great idea can be in the hands of one incompetent to understand it, than the fertility it contained. The merit of Blackstone is his learning, which was substantial, his realization that the powers of law demand some classification, his dim yet constant sense that Montesquieu is right alike in searching for the roots of law in custom and in applying the historical method to his explanations. But as a thinker he was little more than an optimistic trifler, too content with the conditions of his time to question its assumptions.

De Lolme is a more interesting figure; and though, as with Blackstone, what he failed to see was even more remarkable than what he did perceive, his book has real ability and merit. De Lolme was a citizen of Geneva, who published his *Constitution of England* in 1775, after a twelve months' visit to shores sufficiently inhospitable to leave him to die in obscurity and want. His book, as he tells us in his preface, was no mean success, though he derived no profit from it. Like Blackstone, he was impressed by the necessity of obtaining a constitutional equilibrium, wherein he finds the secret of liberty. The attitude was not unnatural in one who, with his head full of Montesquieu, was a witness of the struggle between Junius and the king. He has, of course, the limitation common to all writers before Burke of thinking of government in purely mechanical terms. 'It is upon the passions of mankind,' he says, ' that is, upon causes which are unalterable, that the action of the various parts of a state depends. The machine may vary as to its dimensions; but its movement and acting springs still remain intrinsically the same.' Elsewhere he speaks of government as ' a great ballet or dance in which . . . everything depends upon the disposition of the figures '. He does not deal, that is to say, with men as men, but only as inert adjuncts of a machine by which they are controlled. Such an attitude is bound to suffer from the patent vices of all abstraction. It regards historic forces as distinct from the men related to them. Every mob, he says, must have its Spartacus; every republic will tend to instability. The English avoid these dangers by playing off the royal power against the popular. The king's interest is safeguarded by the division of Parliament into two Houses, each of which rejects the encroachment of the other upon the executive. His power is limited by parliamentary privilege, freedom of the press, the right of taxation and so forth. The theory was not true; though it represented with some accuracy the ideals of the time.

Nor must we belittle what insight De Lolme possessed. He saw that the early concentration of power in the royal hands prevented the continental type of feudalism from developing in England; with the result that while French nobles were massacring each other, the English people could unite to wrest privileges from the superior power. He understood that one of the mainsprings of the system was the independence of the judges. He realized that the party-system—he never used the actual term—while it provides room for men's ambitions at the same time prevents the equation of ambition with indispensability. ' Woe to him ', says De Lolme, '. . . who should endeavour to make the people believe that their fate depends on the persevering virtue of a single citizen.'

He sees the paramount value of freedom of the press. This, as he says, with the necessity that members should be re-elected, 'has delivered into the hands of the people at large the exercise of the censorial power'. He has no doubt but that resistance is the remedy whereby governmental encroachment can be prevented; 'resistance', he says, 'is the ultimate and lawful resource against the violences of power'. He points out how real is the guarantee of liberty where the onus of proof in criminal cases is thrown upon the government. He regards with admiration the supremacy of the civil over the military arm, and the skilful way in which, contrary to French experience, it has been found possible to maintain a standing army without adding to the royal power. Nor can he fail to admire the insight which organizes 'the agitation of the popular mind', not as 'the forerunner of violent commotions' but to 'animate all parts of the state'. Therein De Lolme had grasped the real essence of party government.

It was, of course, no more than symptomatic of his time that Cabinet and Prime Minister should have escaped his notice. A more serious defect was his inability, with the Wilkes contest prominently in his notice, to see that the people had assumed a new importance. For the masses, indeed, De Lolme had no enthusiasm. A passive share, he thought, was the only one that could, with safety to the state, be trusted to the humble man. 'The greater part', he wrote, 'of those who compose this multitude, taken up with the care of providing for their subsistence, have neither sufficient leisure, nor even, in consequence of their imperfect education, that degree of information, requisite for functions of this kind.' Such an attitude blinded him to the significance of the American conflict, which he saw unattended by its moral implications. He trusted too emphatically to the power of mechanisms to realize that institutions which allowed of such manipulation as that of George III could not be satisfactory once the People had awakened to a sense of its own power. The real social forces of the time found there no channels of activity; and the difference between De Lolme and Bagehot is the latter's power to go behind the screen of statute to the inner sources of power.

## IV

The basis of revolutionary doctrine was already present in England when, in 1762, Rousseau published his *Contrat Social*. With its fundamental doctrines Locke had already made his countrymen familiar; and what was needed for the appreciation of its teaching was less a renaissance than discontent. So soon as men are dissatisfied with the traditional foundations of the State, a gospel of natural rights is certain to make its appearance. And, once the design of George III had been made familiar by his treatment of Chatham and Wilkes, the discontent did not fail to show itself. Indeed, in the year before the publication of Rousseau's book, Robert Wallace, a Scottish chaplain-royal, had written in his *Various Prospects* (1761) a series of essays which are at once an anticipation of the main thesis of Malthus and a plea for the integration of social forces by which alone the mass of men could be raised from misery. In the light of later experience it is difficult not to be impressed by the modernist flavour of Wallace's attack. He insists upon the capacity of men and the disproportion between their potential achievement and that which is secured by actual society. Men are in the mass condemned to ignorance and toil; and the lust of power sets man against his neighbour to the profit of the rich. Wallace traces these evils to private property and the individualistic organization of work, and he sees no remedy save community of possessions and a renovated educational system. Yet he does not conceal from himself that it is to the interest of the governing class to prevent a revolution which, beneficent to the masses, would be fatal to themselves; nor does he conceive it possible until the fertility of men has been reduced to the capacity of the soil. He speculates upon the chances of a new spirit among men, of an all-wise legislator, and of the beneficent example of colonies upon the later Owenite model. But his book is contemporaneous with our own ideas rather than with the thoughts of his generation. Nor does it seem to have excited any general attention.

It is five years after Rousseau that we see the first clear signs of his influence. Naturally enough the men amongst whom the new spirit spread abroad were the Nonconformists. For more than seventy years they had been allowed existence without recognition. None had more faithfully supported the new dynasty than they; none had been paid less for their allegiance. Their utmost effort could secure only a sparing mitigation of the Test Act. All of them were Whigs, and the doctrines of Locke suited exactly their temper and their wants. There were amongst them able men in every walk of life, and they were apt to publication. Joseph Priestley, in particular, gave up with willingness to mankind what was obviously meant for chemical science. A few years previously Brown of the *Estimate* had submitted a scheme

for national education, in which the essential principle
was Church control. Priestley had answered him, and
was encouraged by friends to expand his argument into
a general treatise. His *Essay on the First Principles of Government*
appeared in 1768; and, if for nothing else, it would
be noteworthy because it was therein that the significance
of the ' greatest happiness principle ' first flashed across
Bentham's mind. But the book shows more than this.
' I had placed ', says Priestley with due modesty, ' the
foundation of some of the most valuable interests of
mankind on a broader and firmer basis than Mr.
Locke '; and the breadth and firmness are Rousseau's
contribution.

Certainly we herein meet new elements. On the very
threshold of the book we meet the dogma of the perfect-
ibility of man. ' Whatever ', Priestley rhapsodizes, ' was
the beginning of this world, the end will be glorious and
paradisaical, beyond what our imaginations can now
conceive.' ' The instrument of this progress . . . towards
this glorious state ' is government; though a little later
we are to find that the main business of government is
non-interference. Men are all equal, and their natural
rights are indefeasible. Government must be restrained
in the interests of liberty. No man can be governed
without his consent; for government is founded upon a
contract by which civil liberty is surrendered in exchange
for a power to share in public decisions. It thus follows
that the people must be sovereign, and interference with
their natural rights will justify resistance. Every government, he says, is ' in its original principles, and antecedent to its present form an equal republic '; wherefore,
of course, it follows that we must restore to men the
equality they have lost. And, equally, of course, this

would bestow upon the Nonconformists their full citizenship; for Warburton's *Alliance*, to attack which Priestley exhausts all the resources of his ingenuity, has been one of the main instruments in their degradation. 'Unbounded liberty in matters of religion', which means the abolition of the Establishment, promises to be 'very favourable to the best interests of mankind'.

So far the book might well be called an edition of Rousseau for English Nonconformists; but there are divergences of import. It can never be forgotten in the history of political ideas that the alliance of Church and State made Nonconformists suspicious of government interference. Their original desire to be left unimpeded was soon exalted into a definite theory; and since political conditions had confined them so largely to trade, none felt as they did the hampering influence of State restrictions. The result has been a great difficulty in making liberal doctrines in England realize, until after 1870, the organic nature of the State. It remains for them almost entirely a police institution which, once it aims at the realization of right, usurps a function far better performed by individuals. There is no sense of the community; all that exists is a sum of private sentiments. 'Civil liberty', says Priestley, 'has been greatly impaired by an abuse of the maxim that the joint understanding of all the members of a State, properly collected, must be preferable to that of individuals; and consequently that the more the cases are in which mankind are governed by this united reason of the whole community, so much the better; whereas, in truth, the greater part of human actions are of such a nature, that more inconvenience would follow from their being fixed by laws than from their being left to every man's arbitrary will.' If my neighbour assaults me, he suggests, I may usefully call in the police; but where the object is the discovery of truth, the means of education, the method of religious belief, individual initiative is superior to State action. The latter produces a uniform result ' incompatible with the spirit of discovery '. Nor is such attempt at uniform conditions just to posterity; men have no natural right to judge for the future. Men are too ignorant to fix their own ideas as the basis of all action.

Priestley could not escape entirely the bondage of past tradition; and the metaphysics which Bentham abhorred are scattered broadcast over his pages. Nevertheless the basis upon which he defended his ideals was a utilitarianism hardly less complete than that which Bentham made the instrument of revolution. ' Regard to the general good ', he says, ' is the main method by which natural rights are to be defended.' ' The good and happiness of the members, that is, the majority of the members of any State, is the great standard by which everything relating to that State must finally be determined.' In substance, that is to say, if not completely in theory, we pass with Priestley from arguments of right to those of expediency. His chief attack upon religious legislation is similarly based upon considerations of policy. His view of the individual as a never-ending source of fruitful innovation anticipates all the later Benthamite arguments about the well-spring of individual energy. Interference and stagnation are equated in exactly similar fashion to Adam Smith and his followers. Priestley, of course, was inconsistent in urging at the outset that government is the chief instrument of progress; but what he seems to mean is less that government has the future in its hands than that government action may well be decisive for good or evil. Typical, too, of the later Benthamism is his glorification of reason as the great key which is to unlock all doors. That is, of course, natural in a scientist who had himself made discoveries of vital import; but it was characteristic also of a school which scanned a limitless horizon with serene confidence in a future of unbounded good. Even if it be said that Priestley has all the vices of that rationalism which, as with Bentham, over-simplifies every problem it en-counters, it is yet adequate to retort that a confidence in the energies of men was better than the complacent stagnation of the previous age.

It is difficult to measure the precise influence that Priestley exerted; certainly among Nonconformists it cannot have been small. Dr. Richard Price is a lesser figure; and much of the standing he might have had has been obliterated by two unfortunate incidents. His sinking-fund scheme was taken up by the younger Pitt, and proved, though the latter believed in it to the last, to be founded upon an arithmetical fallacy which did not sit well upon a fellow of the Royal Society. His sermon on the French Revolution provoked the *Reflec-tions* of Burke; and, though much of the right was on the side of Price, it can hardly be said that he survived Burke's onslaught. Yet he was a considerable figure in his day, and he shows, like Priestley, how deep-rooted was the English revolutionary temper. He has not, in-deed, Priestley's superb optimism; for the rigid *a priori* morality of which he was the somewhat muddled de-fender was less favourable to a confidence in reason. He had a good deal of John Brown's fear that luxury was the seed of English degeneration; the proof of which he saw in the decline of the population. His figures, in fact, were false; but they were unessential to the general thesis he had to make.

Price, like Priestley a leading Nonconformist, was stirred to print by the American Revolution; and if his views were not widely popular, his *Observations on the Nature of Civil Liberty* (1776) attained its eighth edition within a decade. This, with its supplement *Additional Observations* (1777), presents a perfectly coherent theory. Nor is their ancestry concealed. They represent the tradition of Locke, modified by the importations of Rousseau. Price owes much to Priestley and to Hume, and he takes sentences from Montesquieu where they aid him. But he has little or nothing of Priestley's utilitarianism and the whole argument is upon the abstract basis of right. Liberty means self-government, and self-government means the right of every man to be his own legislator. Price, with strict logic, follows out this doctrine to its last consequence. Taxes become ' free gifts for public services '; laws are ' particular provisions or regulations established by Common Consent for gaining protection and safety '; magistrates are ' trustees or deputies for carrying these regulations into execution '. And almost in the words of Rousseau, Price goes on to admit that liberty, ' in its most perfect degree, can be enjoyed only in small states where every independent agent is capable of giving his suffrage in person and of being chosen into public offices '. He knows that large States are inevitable, though he thinks that representation may be made so adequate as to minimize the sacrifice of liberty involved.

But the limitation upon government is everywhere emphasized. ' Government ', he says, ' . . . is in the very nature of it a trust; and all its powers a Delegation for particular ends.' He rejects the theory of parliamentary sovereignty as incompatible with self-government; if the Parliament, for instance, prolonged its life, it would betray its constituents and dissolve itself. 'If omnipotence', he writes, 'can with any sense be ascribed to a legislature, it must be lodged where all legislative authority originates; that is, in the People.' Such a system is alone compatible with the ends of government, since it cannot be supposed that men 'combine into communities and institute government' for self-enslavement. Nor is any other political system 'consistent with the natural equality of mankind'; by which Price means that no man 'is constituted by the author of nature the vassal or subject of another, or has any right to give law to him, or, without his consent, to take away any part of his property or to abridge him of his liberty'. From all of which it is concluded that liberty is inalienable; and a people which has lost it 'must have a right to emancipate themselves as soon as they can'. The aptness of the argument to the American situation is obvious enough; and nowhere is Price more happy or more formidable than when he applies his precepts to phrases like 'the unity of the empire' and the 'honour of the kingdom', which were so freely used to cover up the inevitable results of George's obstinacy.

The *Essay on the Right of Property in Land* (1781) of William Ogilvie deserves at least a passing notice. The author, who published his book anonymously, was a Professor of Latin in the University of Aberdeen and an agriculturist of some success. His own career was distinctly honourable. The teacher of Sir James Mackintosh, he had a high reputation as a classical scholar and deserves to be remembered for his effort to reform a college which had practically ceased to perform its proper academic functions. His book is virtually an essay upon the natural right of men to the soil. He does not doubt that the distress of the times is due to the land monopoly. The earth being given to men in common, its invasion by private ownership is a dangerous perversion. Men have the right to the full product of their labour; but the privileges of the landowner prevent the enjoyment of that right. The primary duty of every State is the increase of public happiness; and the happiest nation is that which has the greatest number of free and independent cultivators. But governments attend rather to the interest of the higher classes, even while they hold out the protection of the common people as the main pretext of their authority. The result is their maintenance of land-monopoly even though it affects the prime material of all essential industries, prevents the growth of population, and makes the rich wealthier at the expense of the poor. It breeds oppression and ignorance, and poisons improvement by preventing individual initiative. He points out how a nation is dominated by its landlords, and how they have consistently evaded the fiscal burdens they should bear. Only in return to a nation of freeholders can Ogilvie see the real source of an increase in happiness.

Such criticism is revolutionary enough, though when he comes to speak of actual changes, he had little more to propose than a system of peasant proprietorship. What is striking in the book is its sense of great, impending changes, its thorough grasp of the principle of utility, its realization of the immense agricultural improvement that is possible if the landed system can

be so changed as to bring into play the impulses of
humble men. He sees clearly enough that wealth dominates the State; and his interpretation of history is
throughout economic. Ogilvie is one of the first of those
agrarian Socialists who, chiefly through Spence and
Paine, are responsible for a special current of their own
in the great tide of protest against the unjust situation
of labour. Like them, he builds his system upon natural
rights; though, unlike them, his natural rights are defended by expediency and in a style that is always clear
and logical. The book itself has rather a curious history.
At its appearance, it seems to have excited no notice of
any kind. Mackintosh knew of its authorship; for he
warned its author against the amiable delusion that its
excellence would persuade the British government to
force a system of peasant proprietorship upon the East
India Company. Reprinted in 1838 as the work of
John Ogilby, it was intended to instruct the Chartists
in the secret of their oppression; and therein it may
well have contributed to the tragicomic land-scheme of
Feargus O'Connor. In 1891 the problem of the land
was again eagerly debated under the stimulus of Henry
George; and a patriotic Scotsman published the book
with biographical notes that constitute one of the most
amazing curiosities in English political literature.


V


Against the school of Rousseau's English disciples it
is comparatively easy to multiply criticisms. They lacked
any historic sense. Government, for them, was simply an
instrument which was made and unmade at the volition
of men. How complex were its psychological foundations

they had no conception; with the single factor of consent they could explain the most marvellous edifice of any time. They were buried beneath a mountain of meta-physical right which they never related to legal facts or to political possibility. They pursued relentlessly the logical conclusions of the doctrines they abhorred without being willing carefully to investigate the results to which their own doctrines in logic led. They overestimated the extent to which men are willing to occupy themselves with political affairs. They made no proper allowance for the protective armour each social system must acquire by the mere force of prescription. Nor is there sufficient allowance in their attitude for those limiting conditions of circumstance of which every statesman must of necessity take account. They occupy themselves, that is to say, so completely with *staatslehre* that they do not admit the mollifying influence of *politik*. They search for principles of universal right, without the per-ception that a right which is to be universal must necessarily be so general in character as to be useless in its application.

Yet such defects must not blind us to the general rightness of their insight. They were protesting against a system strongly upheld on grounds which now appear to have been simply indefensible. The business of govern-ment had been made the private possession of a privileged class; and eagerness for desirable change was, in the mass, absent from the minds of most men engaged in its direction. The loss of America, the heartless treat-ment of Ireland, the unconstitutional practices in the Wilkes affair, the heightening of corruption undertaken by Henry Fox and North at the direct instance of the king, had blinded the eyes of most to the fact that

principle is a vital part of policy. The revolutionists re-
called men to the need of explaining, no less than
carrying on, the government of the Crown. They represented the new sense of power felt by elements of which
the importance had been forgotten in the sordid intrigues
of the previous half-century. Their emphasis upon
government as in its nature a public trust was at least
accompanied by a useful reminder that, after all, ultimate
power must rest upon the side of the governed. For
twenty years Whigs and Tories alike carried on political
controversy as though no public opinion existed outside
the small circle of the aristocracy. The mob which
made Wilkes its idol was, in a blind and unconscious
way, enforcing the lesson that Price and Priestley had
in mind. For the moment, they were unsuccessful. Cartwright, with his Constitutional Societies, might capture
the support of an eccentric peer like the Duke of Rich-
mond; but the vast majority remained, if irritated, un-
convinced. It needed the realization that the new
doctrines were part of a vaster synthesis which swept
within its purview the fortunes of Europe and America
before they would give serious heed; and even then
they met antagonism with nothing save oppression and
hate. Yet the doctrines remained; for thought, after all,
is killed by reasoned answer alone. And when the first
gusts of war and revolution had passed, the cause for
which they stood was found to have permeated all
classes save that which had all to lose by learning.

We must not, however, commit the error of thinking
of Price and Priestley as representing more than an
important segment of opinion. The opposition to their
theories was not less articulate than their own defence
of them. Some, like Burke, desired a purification of the

existing system; others, like Dr. Johnson, had no sort of sympathy with new-fangled ideas. One thinker, at least, deserves some mention, less for the inherent value of what he had to say, than for the nature of the opinions he expounded. Josiah Tucker, the Dean of Gloucester, has a reputation alike in political and economic inquiry. He represents the sturdy nationalism of Arbuthnot's *John Bull*, the unreasoned prejudice against all foreigners, the hatred of all metaphysics as inconsistent with common sense, the desire to let things be on the ground that the effort after change is worse than the evil of which men complain. His *Treatise on Civil Government* (1781) is in many ways a delightful book, bluff, hardy, full of common sense, with, at times, a quaint humour that is all its own. He had really two objects in view: to deal, in the first place, faithfully with the American problem, and, in the second, to explode the new bubble of Rousseau's followers. The second point takes the form of an examination of Locke, to whom, as Tucker shrewdly saw, the theories of the school may trace their ancestry. He analyses the theory of consent in such fashion as to show that if its adherents could be persuaded to be logical, they would have to admit themselves anarchists. He has no sympathy with the state of nature; the noble savage, on investigation, turns out to be a barbaric creature with a club and scalping knife. Government, he does not doubt, is a trust, or, as he prefers, somewhat oddly, to call it, a quasi-contract; but that does not mean that the actual governors can be dismissed when any eccentric happens to take exception to their views. He has no sympathy with parliamentary reform. Give the mob an increase of power, he says, and nothing is to be expected but outrage and violence. He thinks the

constitution very well as it is, and those who preach the
evils of corruption ought to prove their charges instead
of blasphemously asserting that the voice of the people
is the voice of God.

Upon America Tucker has doctrines all his own. He
does not doubt that the Americans deserve the worst
epithets that can be showered upon them. Their right
to self-government he denies as stoutly as ever George III
himself could have desired. But not for one moment
would he fight them to compel their return to British
allegiance. If the American colonies want to go, let
them by all means cut adrift. They are only a useless
source of expenditure. The trade they represent does
not depend upon allegiance, but upon wants that England
can supply if she keeps shop in the proper way, if, that
is, she makes it to their interest to buy in her market.
Indeed, colonies of all kinds seem to him quite useless.
They ever are, he says, and ever were, ' a drain to and
an incumbrance on the Mother-country, requiring perpetual and expensive nursing in their infancy, and
becoming headstrong and ungovernable in proportion
as they grow up '. All wise relations depend upon self-
interest, and that needs no compulsion. If Gibraltar and
Port Mahon and the rest were given up, the result would
be ' multitudes of places . . . abolished, jobs and contracts
effectually prevented, millions of money saved, universal
industry encouraged, and the influence of the Crown
reduced to that mediocrity it ought to have '. Here is
pure Manchesterism half a century before its time; and
one can imagine the good Dean crustily explaining his
notions to the merchants of Bristol who had just rejected
Edmund Burke for advocating free trade with Ireland.

No word on Toryism would be complete without

mention of Dr. Johnson. Here, indeed, we meet less with opinion than with a set of gloomy prejudices, acceptable only because of the stout honesty of the source from which they come. He thought life a poor thing at the best and took a low view of human nature. 'The notion of liberty', he told the faithful Boswell, 'amuses the people of England and helps to keep off the *tedium vitae*.' The idea of a society properly organized into ranks and societies he always esteemed highly. 'I am a friend to subordination', he said, 'as most conducive to the happiness of society.' He was a Jacobite and Tory to the end. Whiggism was the offspring of the devil, the 'negation of all principle'; and he seems to have implied that it led to atheism, which he regarded as the worst of sins. He did not believe in the honesty of republicans; they levelled down, but were never inclined to level up. Men, he felt, had a part to act in society, and their business was to fulfil their allotted station. Rousseau was a very bad man: 'I would sooner sign a sentence for his transportation than that of any fellow who has gone from the Old Bailey these many years.' Political liberty was worthless; the only thing worth while was freedom in private concerns. He blessed the government in the case of general warrants and thought the power of the Crown too small. Toleration he considered due to an inapt distinction between freedom to think and freedom to talk, and any magistrate 'while he thinks himself right . . . ought to enforce what he thinks'. The American revolt he ascribed to selfish faction; and in his *Taxation No Tyranny* (1775) he defended the British government root and branch upon his favourite ground of the necessity of subordination. He was willing, he said, to love all mankind except an American.

Yet Dr. Johnson was the friend of Burke, and he found pleasure in an acquaintance with Wilkes. Nor, in all his admiration for rank and fortune, is there a single element of meanness. The man who wrote the letter to Lord Chesterfield need never fear the charge of abasement. He knew that there was 'a remedy in human nature that will keep us safe under every form of government'. He defined a courtier in the *Idler* as one 'whose business it is to watch the looks of a being weak and foolish as himself'. Much of what he felt was in part a revolt against the sentimental aspect of contemporary liberalism, in part a sturdy contempt for the talk of degeneracy that men such as Brown had made popular. There is, indeed, in all his political observations a strong sense of the virtue of order, and a perception that the radicalism of the time was too abstract to provide an adequate basis for government. Here, as elsewhere, Johnson hated all speculation which raised the fundamental questions. What he did not see was the important truth that in no age are fundamental questions raised save where the body politic is diseased. Rousseau and Voltaire, even Priestley and Price, require something more for answer than unreasoned prejudice. Johnson's attitude would have been admirable where there were no questions to debate; but where Pelham ruled, or Grenville, or North, it had nothing to contribute. Thought, after all, is the one certain weapon of utility in a different and complex world; and it was because the age refused to look it in the face that it invited the approach of revolution.

## CHAPTER VI

# BURKE

## I

IT is the special merit of the English constitutional system that the king stands outside the categories of political conflict. He is the dignified emollient of an organized quarrel which, at least in theory, is due to the clash of antagonistic principle. The merit, indeed, is largely accidental; and we shall miss the real fashion in which it came to be established unless we remark the vicissitudes through which it has passed. The foreign birth of the first two Hanoverians, the insistent widowhood of Queen Victoria, these rather than deliberate foresight have secured the elevated nullification of the Crown. Yet the first twenty-five years of George III's reign represent the deliberate effort of an obstinate man to stem the progress of fifty years and secure once more the balance of power. Nor was the effort defeated without a struggle which went to the root of constitutional principle.

And George III attempted the realization of his ambition at a time highly favourable to its success. Party government had lost much credit during Walpole's administration. Men like Bolingbroke, Carteret, and the elder Pitt were all of them dissatisfied with a system which depended for its existence upon the exclusion of able men from power. A generation of corrupt practice

and the final defeat of Stuart hopes had already deprived
the Whigs of any special hold on their past ideals. They
were divided already into factions the purpose of which
was no more than the avid pursuit of place and pension.
Government by connexion proved itself irreconcilable
with good government. But it showed also that once
corruption was centralized there was no limit to its
influence, granted only the absence of great questions.
When George III transferred that organization from
the office of the minister to his own court, there was
already a tolerable certainty of his success. For more
than forty years the Tories had been excluded from
office; and they were more than eager to sell their
support. The Church had become the creature of the
State. The drift of opinion in continental Europe was
towards benevolent despotism. The narrow, obstinate,
and ungenerous mind of George had been fed on high
notions of the power he might exert. He had been
taught the kingship of Bolingbroke's glowing picture;
and a reading in manuscript of the seventh chapter of
Blackstone's first book can only have confirmed the
ideals he found there. Nor was it obvious that a genuine
kingship would have been worse than the oligarchy of
the great Whig families.

What made it worse, and finally impossible, was the
character of the king. The pathetic circumstances of
his old age have combined somewhat to obscure the
viciousness of his maturity. He was excessively ignorant
and as obstinate as arbitrary. He trusted no one but
himself, and he totally misunderstood the true nature
of his office. There is no question which arose in the
first forty years of his reign in which he was not upon
the wrong side and proud of his error. He was wrong

about Wilkes, wrong about America, wrong about Ireland, wrong about France. He demanded servants instead of ministers. He attacked every measure for the purification of the political system. He supported the slave trade and he opposed the repeal of the Test Act. He prevented the grant of Catholic emancipation at the one moment when it might have genuinely healed the wounds of Ireland. He destroyed by his perverse creations the value of the House of Lords as a legislative assembly. He was clearly determined to make his will the criterion of policy; and his design might have succeeded had his ability and temper been proportionate to its greatness. It was not likely that the mass of men would have seen with regret the destruction of the aristocratic monopoly in politics. The elder Pitt might well have based a ministry of the court upon a broad bottom of popularity. The House of Commons, as the event proved, could be as subservient to the king as to his minister.

Yet the design failed; and it failed because, with characteristic stupidity, the king did not know the proper instruments for his purpose. Whatever he touched he mismanaged. He aroused the suspicion of the people by enforcing the resignation of the elder Pitt. In the Wilkes affair he threw the clearest light of the century upon the true nature of the House of Commons. His own system of proscription restored to the Whig party not a little of the idealism it had lost; and Burke came to supply them with a philosophy. Chatham remained the idol of the people despite his hatred. He raised Wilkes to be the champion of representative government and of personal liberty. He lost America and it was not his fault that Ireland was retained. The early popularity

he received he never recovered until increasing years
and madness had made him too pathetic for dislike.
The real result of his attempt was to compel attention
once again to the foundations of politics; and George's
effort, in the light of his immense failures, could not,
in the nature of things, survive that analysis.

Not, of course, that George ever lacked defenders. As
early as 1761, the old rival of Walpole, Pulteney, whom
a peerage had condemned to obsolescence, published
his *Seasonable Hints from an Honest Man on the new Reign*.
Pulteney urged the sovereign no longer to be content
with the ' shadow of royalty '. He should use his ' legal
prerogatives ' to check ' the illegal claims of factious
oligarchy '. Government had become the private possession of a few powerful men. The king was but a
puppet in leading strings. The basis of government
should be widened, for every honest man was aware
that distinctions of party were now merely nominal.
The Tories should be admitted to place. They were
now friendly to the accession and they no longer boasted
their hostility to dissent. They knew that Toleration
and the Establishment were of the essence of the constitution. Were once the Whig oligarchy overthrown
corruption would cease and Parliament could no longer
hope to dominate the kingdom. ' The ministers ', he
said, ' will depend on the Crown not the Crown on
ministers ' if George but showed ' his resolution to break
all factitious connexions and confederacies '. The tone
is Bolingbroke's, and it was the lesson George had in-
sistently heard from early youth. How sinister was the
advice, men did not see until the elder Pitt was in
exile, with Wilkes an outlaw, and general warrants
threatening the whole basis of past liberties.

The first writer who pointed out in unmistakable
terms the meaning of the new synthesis was Junius.
That his anonymity concealed the malignant talent of
Sir Philip Francis seems now beyond denial. Junius,
indeed, can hardly claim a place in the history of political
ideas. His genius lay not in the discussion of principle
but the dissection of personality. His power lay in his
style, and the knowledge that enabled him to inform
the general public of facts which were the private
possession of the inner political circle. His mind was
narrow and pedantic. He stood with Grenville on
American taxation; and he maintained without perceiving what it meant that a nomination borough was
a freehold beyond the competence of the legislature to
abolish. He was never generous, always abusive, and
truth did not enter into his calculations. But he saw
with unsurpassed clearness the nature of the issue and
he was a powerful instrument in the discomfiture of the
king. He won a new audience for political conflict and
that audience was the unenfranchised populace of England. His letters, moreover, appearing as they did in
the daily journals, gave the press a significance in politics
which it has never lost. He made the significance of
George's effort known to the mass of men at a time
when no other means of information was at hand. The
opposition was divided; the king's friends were in a vast
majority; the publication of debates was all but impossible. English government was a secret conflict in
which the entrance of spectators was forbidden even
though they were the subjects of debate. It was the
glory of Junius that he destroyed that system. Not even
the combined influence of the Crown and Commons,
not even Lord Mansfield's doctrine of the law of libel,

K

could break the power of his vituperation and Wilkes's courage. Bad men have sometimes been the instruments of noble destiny; and there are few more curious episodes in English history than the result of this alliance between revengeful hate and insolent ambition.

## II

Yet, in the long run, the real weapon which defeated George was the ideas of Edmund Burke; for he gave to the political conflict its real place in philosophy. There is no immortality save in ideas; and it was Burke who gave a permanent form to the debate in which he was the liberal protagonist. His career is illustrative at once of the merits and defects of English politics in the eighteenth century. The son of an Irish Protestant lawyer and a Catholic mother, he served, after learning what Trinity College, Dublin, could offer him, a long apprenticeship to politics in the upper part of Grub Street. The story that he applied, along with Hume, for Adam Smith's chair at Glasgow seems apocryphal; though the *Dissertation on the Sublime and the Beautiful* (1756) shows his singular fitness for the studies that Hutcheson had made the special possession of the Scottish school. It was in Grub Street that he appears to have attained that amazing amount of varied yet profound knowledge which made him without equal in the House of Commons. His earliest production was *A Vindication of Natural Society* (1756), written in the manner of Lord Bolingbroke, and successful enough in its imitative satire not only to deceive its immediate public, but also to become the basis of Godwin's *Political Justice*. After a vain attempt to serve in Ireland with ' Single-Speech ' Hamilton, he became the private secretary to Lord Rockingham, the leader of the one section of the Whig party to which an honourable record still remained. That connexion secured for him a seat in Parliament at the comparatively late age of thirty-six; and henceforward, until his death in 1797, he was among its leading members. His intellectual pre-eminence, indeed, seems from the very outset to have been recognized on all hands; though he was still, in the eyes of the system, enough of an outsider to be given, in the short months during which he held office, the minor office of Paymaster-General, without a seat in the Cabinet. The man of whom all England was the political pupil was denied without discussion a place at the council board. Yet when Fox is little more than a memory of great lovableness and Pitt a marvellous youth of apt quotations, Burke has endured as the permanent manual of political wisdom without which statesmen are as sailors on an uncharted sea.

For it has been the singular good fortune of Burke not merely to obtain acceptance as the apostle of philosophic conservatism, but to give deep comfort to men of liberal temper. He is, indeed, a singularly lovable figure. ' His stream of mind is perpetual ', said Johnson; and Goldsmith has told us how he wound his way into a subject like a serpent. Macaulay thought him the greatest man since Milton, Lord Morley the ' greatest master of civil wisdom in our tongue '. ' No English writer ', says Sir Leslie Stephen, ' has received or has deserved more splendid panegyrics.' Even when the last criticism has been made, detraction from these estimates is impossible. It is easy to show how irritable and violent was his temperament. There is evidence and to spare of the way in which he allowed the spirit of party to cloud his judgement. His relations with Lord Chatham give lamentable proof of the violence of his personal antipathies. As an orator, his speeches are often turgid, wanting in self-control, and full of those ample digressions in which Gladstone delighted to obscure his principles. Yet the irritation did not conceal a magnificent loyalty to his friends, and it was in his days of comparative poverty that he shared his means with Barry and with Crabbe. His alliance with Fox is the classic partnership in English politics, unmarred, even enriched, by the tragedy of its close. He was never guilty of mean ambition. He thought of nothing save the public welfare. No man has ever more consistently devoted his energies to the service of the nation with less regard for personal advancement. No English statesman has ever more firmly moved amid a mass of details to the principle they involve.

He was a member of no school of thought, and there is no influence to whom his outlook can be directly traced. His politics, indeed, bear upon their face the preoccupation with the immediate problems of the House of Commons. Yet through them all the principles that emerge form a consistent whole. Nor is this all. He hated oppression with all the passion of a generous moral nature. He cared for the good as he saw it with a steadfastness which Bright and Cobden only can claim to challenge. What he had to say he said in sentences which form the maxims of administrative wisdom. His horizon reached from London out to India and America; and he cared as deeply for the Indian ryot's wrongs as for the iniquities of English policy to Ireland. With less width of mind than Hume and less intensity of gaze than Adam Smith, he yet had a width and intensity which, fused with his own imaginative sympathy, gave him more insight than either. He had an unerring eye for the eternal principles of politics. He knew that ideals must be harnessed to an Act of Parliament if they are not to cease their influence. Admitting while he did that politics must rest upon expediency, he never failed to find good reason why expediency should be identified with what he saw as right. It is a stainless and a splendid record. There are men in English politics to whom a greater immediate influence may be ascribed, just as in political philosophy he cannot claim the persistent inspiration of Hobbes and Locke. But in that middle ground between the facts and speculation his supremacy is unapproached. There had been nothing like him before in English politics; and in continental politics Royer-Collard alone has something of his moral fibre, though his practical insight was far less profound. Hamilton had Burke's full grasp of political wisdom, but he lacked his moral elevation. So that he remains a figure of uniqueness. He may, as Goldsmith said, have expended upon his party talents that should have illuminated the universal aspect of the State. Yet there is no question with which he dealt that he did not leave the richer for his inquiry.

## III

The liberalism of Burke is most apparent in his handling of the immediate issues of the age. Upon Ireland, America, and India, he was at every point upon the side of the future. Where constitutional reform was in debate no man saw more clearly than he the evils that needed remedy; though, to a later generation, his

own schemes bear the mark of timid conservatism. In
the last decade of his life he encountered the greatest
cataclysm unloosed upon Europe since the Reformation,
and it is not too much to say that at every point he
missed the essence of its meaning. Yet even upon France
and the English constitution he was full of practical
sagacity. Had his warning been uttered without the
fury of hate that accompanied it, he might well have
guided the forces of the Revolution into channels that
would have left no space for the military dictatorship
he so marvellously foresaw. Had he perceived the real
evils of the aristocratic monopoly against which he so
eloquently inveighed, forty barren years might well
have been a fruitful epoch of wise and continuous reform.
But Burke was not a democrat, and, at bottom, he had
little regard for that popular sense of right which, upon
occasion, he was ready to praise. What impressed
him was less the evils of the constitution than its possibilities, could the defects quite alien from its nature
but be pruned away. Moments, indeed, there are of a
deeper vision, and it is not untrue to say that the best
answer to Burke's conservatism is to be found in his own
pages. But he was too much the apostle of order to
watch with calm the struggle involved in the overthrow
of privilege. He had too much the sense of a Divine
Providence taking thought for the welfare of men to
interfere with violence in his handiwork. The tinge of
caution is never absent, even from his most liberal
moments; and he was willing to endure great evil if it
seemed dangerous to estimate the cost of change.

His American speeches are the true text-book for
colonial administration. He put aside the empty plea
of right which satisfied legal pedants like George Gren-

ville. What moved him was the tragic fashion in which
men clung to the shadow of a power they could not
maintain instead of searching for the roots of freedom.
He never concealed from himself that the success of
America was bound up with the maintenance of English
liberties. 'Armies,' he said many years later, 'first
victorious over Englishmen, in a conflict for English
constitutional rights and privileges, and afterwards
habituated (though in America) to keep an English
people in a state of abject subjection, would prove fatal
in the end to the liberties of England itself.' He had firm
hold of that insidious danger which belittles freedom
itself in the interest of curtailing some special desire.
'In order to prove that the Americans have no right
to their liberties,' he said in the famous *Speech on Conciliation with America* (1775), 'we are every day en-
deavouring to subvert the maxims which preserve the
whole spirit of our own.' The way for the later despotism
of the younger Pitt, was, as Burke saw, prepared by those
who persuaded Englishmen of the paltry character of
the American contest. His own receipt was sounder. In
the *Speech on American Taxation* (1774) he had riddled the
view that the fiscal methods of Lord North were likely
to succeed. The true method was to find a way of peace.
'Nobody shall persuade me,' he told a hostile House of
Commons, 'when a whole people are concerned, that
acts of lenity are not means of conciliation.' 'Mag-
nanimity in politics', he said in the next year, 'is not
seldom the truest wisdom; and a great empire and little
minds go ill together.' He did not know, in the most
superb of all his maxims, how to draw up an indictment
against a whole people. He would win the colonies by
binding them to England with the ties of freedom.

' The question with me ', he said, ' is not whether you have a right to render your people miserable, but whether it is not your interest to make them happy.' The problem, in fact, was one not of abstract right but of expediency; and nothing could be lost by satisfying American desire. Save for Johnson and Gibbon, that was apparent to every first-class mind in England. But the obstinate king prevailed; and Burke's great protest remained no more than material for the legislation of the future. Yet it was something that ninety years after his speech the British North America Act should have given his dreams full substance.

Ireland had always a place apart in Burke's affections, and when he first entered the House of Commons he admitted that uppermost in his thoughts was the desire to assist its freedom. He saw that here, as in America, no man will be argued into slavery. A government which defied the fundamental impulses of men was bound to court disaster. How could it seek security where it defied the desires of the vast majority of its subjects? Why is the Irish Catholic to have less justice than the Catholic of Quebec or the Indian Mohammedan? The system of Protestant control, he said, in the *Letter to Sir Hercules Langrishe* (1792), was ' well fitted for the oppression, impoverishment and degradation of a people, and the debasement in them of human nature itself'. The Catholics paid their taxes; they served with glory in the army and navy. Yet they were denied a share in the commonwealth. ' Common sense ', he said, ' and common justice dictate . . . some sort of compensation to a people for their slavery.' The British constitution was not made ' for great, general and proscriptive exclusions; sooner or later it will destroy them, or they will destroy the constitution'. The argument that the body of Catholics was prone to sedition was no reason to oppress them. ' No man will assert seriously ', he said, ' that when people are of a turbulent spirit the best way to keep them in order is to furnish them with something to complain of.' The advantages of subjects were, as he urged, their right; and a wise government would regard ' all their reasonable wishes as so many claims '. To neglect them was to have a nation full of uneasiness; and the end was bound to be disaster.

There is nothing more noble in Burke's career than his long attempt to mitigate the evils of Company rule in India. Research may well have shown that in some details he pressed the case too far; yet nothing has so far come to light to cast doubt upon the principles he there maintained. He was the first English statesman fully to understand the moral import of the problem of subject races; and if he did not make impossible the Joseph Sedleys of the future, at least he flung an eternal challenge to their malignant complacency. He did not ask the abandonment of British dominion in India, though he may have doubted the wisdom of its conquest. All that he insisted upon was this, that in imperial adventure the conquering race must abide by a moral code. A lie was a lie whether its victim be black or white. The European must respect the powers and rights of the Hindu as he would be compelled by law to respect them in his own State. ' If we are not able ', he said, ' to contrive some method of governing India well which will not of necessity become the means of governing Great Britain ill, a ground is laid for their eternal separation, but none for sacrificing the people of that country to our constitution.' England must be in India for India's benefit or not at all; political power and commercial monopoly such as the East India Company enjoyed could be had only in so far as they are instruments of right and not of violence. The Company's system was the antithesis of this. 'There is nothing', he said in a magnificent passage, 'before the eyes of the natives but an endless, hopeless prospect of new flights of birds of prey and passage, with appetites continually renewing for a food that is continually wasting.' Sympathy with the native, regard for his habits and wants, the Company's servants failed to display. 'The English youth in India drink the intoxicating draught of authority and dominion before their heads are able to bear it, and as they are full grown in fortune long before they are ripe in principle, neither nature nor reason have any opportunity to exert themselves for the excesses of their premature power. The consequences of their conduct, which in good minds (and many of theirs are probably such) might produce penitence or amendment, are unable to pursue the rapidity of their flight. Their prey is lodged in England; and the cries of India are given to seas and winds to be blown about in every breaking up of the monsoon over a remote and unhearing ocean.' More than a century was to pass before the wisest of Burke's interpreters attempted the translation of his maxims into statute. But there has never, in any language, been drawn a clearer picture of the danger implicit in imperial adventure. 'The situation of man', said Burke, 'is the preceptor of his duty.' He saw how a nation might become corrupted by the spoils of other lands. He knew that cruelty abroad is the parent of a later cruelty at home. Men will complain of their wrongdoing in the remoter empire; and imperialism will employ the means

Burke painted in unforgettable terms in his picture of
Paul Benfield. He denied that the government of subject
races can be regarded as a commercial transaction. Its
problem was not to secure dividends but to accomplish
moral benefit. He abhorred the politics of prestige. He
knew the difficulties involved in administering distant
territories, the ignorance and apathy of the public,
the consequent erosion of responsibility, the chance that
wrong will fail of discovery. But he did not shrink from
his conclusion. ' Let us do what we please ', he said,
' to put India from our thoughts, we can do nothing to
separate it from our public interest and our national
reputation.' That is a general truth not less in Africa
and China than in India itself. The main thought in
Burke's mind was the danger lest colonial dominion
become the breeding-ground of arbitrary ideas. That
his own safeguards were inadequate is clear enough at
the present time. He knew that the need was good
government. He did not nor could he realize how intimately that ideal was connected with self-government.
Yet the latest lesson is no more than the final outcome
of his teaching.

## IV

A background so consistent as this in the inflexible
determination to moralize political action resulted in
a noble edifice. Yet, through it all, the principles of
policy are rather implied than admitted. It was when
he came to deal with domestic problems and the French
Revolution that Burke most clearly showed the real trend
of his thought. That trend is unmistakable. Burke was
a utilitarian who was convinced that what was old

was valuable by the mere fact of its arrival at maturity. The State appeared to him an organic compound that came but slowly to its full splendour. It was easy to destroy; creation was impossible. Political philosophy was nothing for him but accurate generalization from experience; and he held the presumption to be against novelty. While he did not belittle the value of reason, he was always impressed by the immense part played by prejudice in the determination of policy. He had no doubt that property was a rightful index to power; and to disturb prescription seemed to him the opening of the flood gates. Nor must we miss the religious aspect of his philosophy. He never doubted that religion was the foundation of the English State. ' Englishmen ', he said in the *Reflections on the French Revolution* (1790), ' know, and what is better, we feel inwardly, that religion is the basis of civil society and the source of all good and of all comfort.' The utterance is characteristic, not merely in its depreciation of reason, but in its ultimate reliance upon a mystic explanation of social facts. Nothing was more alien from Burke's temper than deductive thinking in politics. The only safeguard he could find was in empiricism.

This hatred of abstraction is, of course, the basis of his earliest publication; but it remained with him to the end. He would not discuss America in terms of right. ' I do not enter into these metaphysical distinctions;' he said in the *Speech on American Taxation*, ' I hate the very sound of them.' ' One sure symptom of an ill-conducted state ', he wrote in the *Reflections*, ' is the propensity of the people to resort to theories.' ' It is always to be lamented,' he said in a *Speech on the Duration of Parliament*, ' when men are driven to search into the foundations of the commonwealth.' The theory of a social contract he declared ' at best a confusion of judicial with civil principles ', and he found no sense in the doctrine of popular sovereignty. ' The lines of morality ', he said in the *Appeal from the New to the Old Whigs* (1791), ' are not like ideal lines of mathematics. They are broad and deep as well as long. They admit of exceptions; they demand modifications. These exceptions and modifications are made, not by the process of logic but by the rules of prudence. Prudence is not only first in rank of the virtues political and moral, but she is the director, the regulator, the standard of them all.' Nor did he hesitate to draw the obvious conclusion. ' This ', he said, ' is the true touchstone of all theories which regard man and the affairs of men—does it suit his nature in general, does it suit his nature as modified by his habits?'

Of the truth of this general attitude it is difficult to make denial. But when Burke came to apply it to the British constitution, the ' rules of prudence ' he was willing to admit are narrow enough to cause surprised inquiry. He did not doubt that the true end of a legislature was ' to give a direction, a form, a technical dress . . . to the general sense of the community '; he admitted that popular revolt is so much the outcome of suffering that in any dispute between government and people, the presumption is at least equal in the latter's favour. He urged the acceptance of Grenville's Bill for improving the method of decision upon disputed elections. He made a magnificent defence of the popular cause in the Middlesex election. He was in favour of the publication of parliamentary debates and of the voting lists in divisions. He supported almost with passion the

ending of that iniquitous system by which the en-
franchisement of revenue officers gave government a
corrupt reservoir of electoral support. His *Speech on
Economical Reform* (1780) was the prelude to a nobly-
planned and successful attack upon the waste of the
civil list.

Yet beyond these measures Burke could never be persuaded to go. He was against the demand for shorter
parliaments on the excellent ground that the elections
would be more corrupt and the Commons less responsible.
He opposed the remedy of a Place Bill for the good and
sufficient reason that it gave the executive an interest
against the legislature. He would not, as in the great
speech at Bristol (1774), accept the doctrine that a
member of Parliament was a mere delegate of his
constituents rather than a representative of his own
convictions. 'Government and legislation', he said,
'are matters of reason and of judgement'; and once
the private member had honourably arrived at a decision which he thought was for the interest of the
whole community, his duty was done. All this, in itself,
is unexceptionable; and it shows Burke's admirable
grasp of the practical application of attractive theories
to the event. But it is to be read in conjunction with a
general hostility to basic constitutional change which
is more dubious. He had no sympathy with the Radicals.
'The bane of the Whigs', he said, 'has been the admission among them of the corps of schemers . . . who
do us infinite mischief by persuading many sober and
well-meaning people that we have designs inconsistent
with the Constitution left us by our forefathers.' 'If the
nation at large', he wrote in another letter, 'has disposition enough to oppose all bad principles and all

bad men, its form of government is, in my opinion,
fully sufficient for it; but if the general disposition be
against a virtuous and manly line of public conduct,
there is no form into which it can be thrown that will
improve its nature or add to its energy '; and in the
same letter he foreshadows a possible retirement from
the House of Commons as a protest against the growth
of radical opinion in his party. He resisted every effort
to reduce the suffrage qualification. He had no sympathy with the effort either to add to the county representation or to abolish the rotten boroughs. The frame-
work of the parliamentary system seemed to him excellent. He deplored all criticism of Parliament, and
even the discussion of its essentials. ' Our representation ', he said, ' is as nearly perfect as the necessary
imperfections of human affairs and of human creatures
will suffer it to be.' It was in the same temper that he
resisted all efforts at the political relief of the Protestant
dissenters. ' The machine itself ', he had said, ' is well
enough to answer any good purpose, provided the
materials were sound '; and he never moved from that
opinion.

Burke's attitude was obsolete even while he wrote;
yet the suggestiveness of his very errors makes examination of their ground important. Broadly, he was protesting against natural right in the name of expediency.
His opponents argued that, since men are by nature
equal, it must follow that they have an equal right to
self-government. To Burke, the admission of this principle
would have meant the overthrow of the British constitution. Its implication was that every institution not
of immediate popular origin should be destroyed. To
secure their ends, he thought, the Radicals were com-

pelled to preach the injustice of those institutions and
thus to injure that affection for government upon which
peace and security depend. Here was an effort to bring
all institutions to the test of logic, which he thought
highly dangerous. ' No rational man ever did govern
himself ', he said, ' by abstractions and universals.' The
question for him was not the abstract rightness of the
system upon some set of *a priori* principles but whether,
on the whole, that system worked for the happiness of
the community. He did not doubt that it did; and to
overthrow a structure so nobly tested by the pressure
of events in favour of some theories outside historic
experience seemed to him ruinous to society. Government, for him, was the general harmony of diverse interests; and the continual adjustments and exquisite
modifications of which it stood in need were admirably
discovered in the existing system. Principles were thus
unimportant compared with the problem of their
application. ' The major ', he said of all political premisses, ' make a pompous figure in the battle, but the
victory depends upon the little minor of circumstances.'

To abstract natural right he therefore opposed prescription. The presumption of wisdom is on the side of
the past, and when we change, we act at our peril.
' Prescription ', he said in 1782, ' is the most solid of all
titles, not only to property, but to what is to secure
that property, to government.' Because he saw the State
organically he was impressed by the smallness both of
the present moment and the individual's thought. It is
built upon the wisdom of the past for ' the species is
wise, and when time is given to it, as a species it almost
always acts right '. And since it is the past alone which
has had the opportunity to accumulate this rightness,

our disposition should be to preserve all ancient things. They could not be without a reason; and that reason is grounded upon ancestral experience. So the prescriptive title becomes ' not the creature, but the master, of positive law . . . the soundest, the most general and the most recognized title between man and man that is known in municipal or public jurisprudence '. It is by prescription that he defends the existence of Catholicism in Ireland not less than the supposed deformities of the British constitution. So, too, his main attack on atheism is its implication that ' everything is to be discussed '. He does not say that all which is has rightness in it; but at least he urges that to doubt it is to doubt the construction of a past experience which built according to the general need. Nor does he doubt the chance that what he urges may be wrong. Rather does he insist that at least it gives us security, for him the highest good. ' Truth ', he said, ' may be far better . . . but as we have scarcely ever that certainty in the one that we have in the other, I would, unless the truth were evident indeed, hold fast to peace, which has in her company charity, the highest of the virtues.'

Such a philosophy, indeed, so barely stated, would seem a defence of political immobility; but Burke attempted safeguards against that danger. His insistence upon the superior value of past experience was balanced by a general admission that particular circumstances must always govern the immediate decision. ' When the reason of old establishments is gone,' he said in his *Speech on Economical Reform*, ' it is absurd to preserve nothing but the burden of them.' ' A disposition to preserve and an ability to improve,' he wrote in the *Reflections on the French Revolution*, ' taken together would

L

be my standard of a statesman.' But that ' ability to improve ' conceals two principles of which Burke never relaxed his hold. ' All the reformations we have hitherto made ', he said, ' have proceeded upon the principle of reference to antiquity '; and the *Appeal from the New to the Old Whigs*, which is the most elaborate exposition of his general attitude, proceeds upon the general basis that 1688 is a perpetual model for the future. Nor is this all. ' If I cannot reform with equity,' said Burke, ' I will not reform at all '; and equity seems here to mean a sacrifice of the present and its passionate demands to the selfish errors of past policy.

Burke, indeed, was never a democrat, and that is the real root of his philosophy. He saw the value of the party-system, and he admitted the necessity of some degree of popular representation. But he was entirely satisfied with current Whig principles, could they but be purged of their grosser deformities. He knew too well how little reason is wont to enter into the formation of political opinion to make the sacrifice of innovation to its power. He saw so much of virtue in the old order, that he insisted upon the equation of virtue with quintessence. Men of great property and position using their influence as a public trust, delicate in their sense of honour, and acting only from motives of right—these seemed to him the men who should with justice exercise political power. He did not doubt that ' there is no qualification for government but virtue and wisdom . . . wherever they are actually found, they have, in whatever state, condition, profession or trade, the passport to heaven '; but he is careful to dissociate the possibility that they can be found in those who practice the mechanical arts. He did not mean that his aristocracy should govern without response to popular demand. He had no objection to criticism, nor to the public exercise of government. There was no reason even for agreement, so long as each party was guided by an honourable sense of the public good. This, so he urged, was the system which underlay the temporary evils of the British constitution. An aristocracy delegated to do its work by the mass of men was the best form of government his imagination could conceive. It meant that property must be dominant in the system of government; that, while office should be open to all, it should be out of the reach of most. ' The characteristic essence of property ', he wrote in the *Reflections*, '. . . is to be unequal '; and he thought the perpetuation of that inequality by inheritance ' that which tends most to the perpetuation of society itself '. The system was difficult to maintain, and it must be put out of the reach of popular temptation. ' Our constitution ', he said in the *Present Discontents*, ' stands on a nice equipoise, with sharp precipices and deep waters on all sides of it. In removing it from a dangerous leaning towards one side, there may be a danger towards oversetting it on the other.' In straining, that is to say, after too large a purification, we may end with destruction. And Burke, of course, was emphatic upon the need that property should be undisturbed. It was always, he thought, at a great disadvantage in any struggle with ability; and there are many passages in which he urges the consequential special representation which the adequate defence of property requires.

The argument, at bottom, is common to all thinkers over-impressed by the sanctity of past experience. Hegel and Savigny in Germany, Taine and Renan in France,

Sir Henry Maine and Lecky in England, have all urged
what is in effect a similar plea. We must not break what
Bagehot called the cake of custom, for men have been
trained to its digestion, and new food breeds trouble.
Laws are the offspring of the original genius of a people,
and while we may renovate, we must not unduly reform.
The true idea of national development is always latent
in the past experience of the race and it is from that
perpetual spring alone that wisdom can be drawn. We
render obedience to what is with effortless unconscious-
ness; and without this loyalty to inherited institutions
the fabric of society would be dissolved. Civilization,
in fact, depends upon the performance of actions defined
in preconceived channels; and if we obeyed those novel
impulses of right which seem, at times, to contradict our
inheritance, we should disturb beyond repair the intricate equilibrium of countless ages. The experience of
the past rather than the desires of the present is thus
the true guide to our policy. ' We ought ', he said in a
famous sentence, ' to venerate where we are unable
presently to comprehend.'

It is easy to see why a mind so attuned recoiled from
horror at the French Revolution. There is something
almost sinister in the destiny which confronted Burke
with the one great spectacle of the eighteenth century
which he was certain not merely to misunderstand but
also to hate. He could not endure the most fragmentary
change in tests of religious belief; and the Revolution
swept overboard the whole religious edifice. He would
not support the abolition even of the most flagrant
abuses in the system of representation; and he was to
see in France an overthrow of a monarchy even more
august in its prescriptive rights than the English Parlia-

ment. Privileges were scattered to the winds in a single night. Peace was sacrificed to exactly those metaphysical theories of equality and justice which he most deeply abhorred. The doctrine of progress found an eloquent defender in that last and noble utterance of Condorcet which is still perhaps its most perfect justification. On all hands there was the sense of a new world built by the immediate thought of man upon the whole-hearted rejection of past history. Politics was emphatically declared to be a system of which the truths could be stated in terms of mathematical certainty. The religious spirit which Burke was convinced lay at the root of good gave way before a general scepticism which, from the outset of life, he had declared incompatible with social order. Justice was asserted to be the centre of social right; and it was defined as the overthrow of those pre-scriptive privileges which Burke regarded as the protective armour of the body politic. Above all, the men who seized the reins of power became convinced that theirs was a specific of universal application. Their disciples in England seemed in the same diabolic frenzy with themselves. In a moment of time, the England which had been the example to Europe of ordered popular liberty became, for these enthusiasts, only less barbaric than the despotic princes of the Continent. That Price and Priestley should suffer the infection was, even for Burke, a not unnatural thing. But when Charles Fox cast aside the teaching of twenty years for its antithesis, Burke must have felt that no price was too great to pay for the overthrow of the Revolution.

Certainly his pamphlets on events in France are at every point consistent with his earlier doctrine. The charge that he supported the Revolution in America

and deserted it in France is without meaning; for in the
one there is no word that can honourably be twisted to
support the other. And when we make allowances for
the grave errors of personal taste, the gross exaggeration,
the inability to see the Revolution as something more
than a single point in time, it becomes obvious enough
that his criticism, de Maistre's apart, is by far the
soundest we possess from the generation which knew
the movement as a living thing. The attempt to produce
an artificial equality upon which he seized as the essence
of the Revolution was, as Mirabeau was urging in private
to the king, the inevitable precursor of dictatorship. He
realized that freedom is born of a certain spontaneity
for which the rigid lines of doctrinaire thinkers left no
room. That worship of symmetrical form which underlies the constitutional experiments of the next few years
he exposed in a sentence which has in it the essence of
political wisdom. ' The nature of man is intricate;' he
wrote in the *Reflections*, ' the objects of society are of the
greatest possible complexity; and therefore no simple
disposition or direction of power can be suitable either
to man's nature or to the quality of his affairs.' The
note recurs in substance throughout his criticism. Much
of its application, indeed, will not stand for one moment
the test of inquiry; as when, for instance, he correlates
the monarchical government of France with the English
constitutional system and extols the perpetual virtues of
1688. The French made every effort to find the secret
of English principles, but the roots were absent from
their national experience.

A year after the publication of the *Reflections* he himself perceived the narrowness of that judgement. In the
*Thoughts on French Affairs* (1791) he saw that the essence

of the Revolution was its foundation in theoretic dogma. It was like nothing else in the history of the world except the Reformation; which last event it especially resembles in its genius for self-propagation. Herein he has already envisaged the importance of that *patrie intellectuelle* which Tocqueville emphasized as born of the Revolution. That led Burke once again to insist upon the peculiar genius of each separate State, the difficulties of a change, the danger of grafting novelties upon an ancient fabric. He saw the certainty that in adhering to an abstract metaphysical scheme the French were in truth omitting human nature from their political equation; for general ideas can find embodiment in institutional forms only after they have been moulded by a thousand varieties of circumstance. The French created a universal man not less destructive of their practical sagacity than the Frankenstein of the economists. They omitted, as Burke saw, the elements which objective experience must demand; with the result that, despite themselves, they came rather to destroy than to fulfil. Napoleon, as Burke prophesied, reaped the harvest of their failure.

Nor was he less right in his denunciation of that distrust of the past which played so large a part in the revolutionary consciousness. ' We are afraid ', he wrote in the *Reflections*, ' to put men to live and trade each on his own private stock of reason, because we suspect that this stock in each man is small, and that the individuals would do better to avail themselves of the general bank and capital of nations and of ages.' Of Siéyès's building constitutions overnight, this is no unfair picture; but it points a more general truth never long absent from Burke's mind. Man is for him so much the creature of prejudice, so much a mosaic of ancestral tradition, that the chance of novel thought finding a peaceful place among his institutions is always small. For Burke, thought is always at the service of the instincts, and these lie buried in the remote experience of the State. So that men like Robespierre were asking from their subjects an impossible task. That which they had conceived in the grey abstractness of their speculations was too little related to what the average Frenchman knew and desired to be enduring. Burke looks with sober admiration at the way in which the English revolution related itself at every point to ideas and theories with which the average man was as familiar as with the physical landmarks of his own neighbourhood. For the motives which underlie all human effort are, he thought, sufficiently constant to compel regard. That upon which they feed submits to change; but the effort is slow and the disappointments many. The Revolution taught the populace the thirst for power. But it failed to remember that sense of continuity in human effort without which new constructions are built on sand. The power it exercised lacked that horizon of the past through which alone it suffers limitation to right ends.

The later part of Burke's attack upon the Revolution does not belong to political philosophy. No man is more responsible than he for the temper which drew England into war. He came to write rather with the zeal of a fanatic waging a holy war than in the temper of a statesman confronted with new ideas. Yet even the *Letters on a Regicide Peace* (1796) have flashes of the old, incomparable insight; and they show that even in the midst of his excesses he did not war for love of it. So that it is permissible to think he did not lightly pen those sentences on peace which stand as oases of wisdom in a desert of extravagant rhetoric. ' War never leaves where it found a nation,' he wrote, ' it is never to be entered upon without mature deliberation.' That was a lesson his generation had still to learn; nor did it take to heart the even nobler passage that follows. ' The blood of man ', he said, ' should never be shed but to redeem the blood of man. It is well shed for our family, for our friends, for our God, for our country, for mankind. The rest is vanity; the rest is crime.' It is perhaps the most tragic wrong in that century's history that these words were written to justify an effort of which they supply an irrefutable condemnation.

V

Criticism of Burke's theories can be made from at least two angles. It is easy to show that his picture of the British constitution was remote from the facts even when he wrote. Every change that he opposed was essential to the security of the next generation; and there followed none of the disastrous consequences he had foreshadowed. Such criticism would be at almost every point just; and yet it would fail to touch the heart of Burke's position. What is mainly needed is analysis at once of his omissions and of the underlying assumptions of what he wrote. Burke came to his maturity upon the eve of the Industrial Revolution; and we have it upon the authority of Adam Smith himself that no one had so clearly apprehended his own economic principles. Yet there is no word in what Burke had to say of their significance. The vast agrarian changes of the time contained, as it appears, no special moment even for him who burdened himself unduly to restore the Beaconsfield estate. No man was more eager than he that the public should be admitted to the mysteries of political debate; yet he steadfastly refused to draw the obvious inference that once the means of government were made known, those who possessed the knowledge would demand their share in its application. He did not see that the metaphysics he so profoundly distrusted was itself the offspring of that contemptible worship of expediency which Blackstone generalized into a legalistic jargon. Men never move to the adumbration of general right until the conquest of political rights has been proved inadequate. That Burke himself may be said in a sense to have seen when he insisted upon the danger of examining the foundations of the State. Yet a man who refuses to admit that the constant dissatisfaction with those foundations which his age expressed is the expression of serious ill in the body politic, is wilfully blind to the facts at issue. No one had more faithfully than Burke himself explained why the Whig oligarchy was obsolete; yet nothing would induce him ever to realize that the alternative to aristocratic government is democracy and that its absence was the cause of that disquiet of which he realized that Wilkes was but the symptom.

Broadly, that is to say, Burke would not realize that the reign of political privilege was drawing to its close. That is the real meaning of the French Revolution and therein it represents a stream of tendency not less active in England than abroad. In France, indeed, the lines were more sharply drawn than elsewhere. The rights men craved were not, as Burke insisted, the immediate offspring of metaphysic fancy, but the result of a determination to end the malignant wrong of centuries. A

power that knew no responsibility, war and intolerance
that derived only from the accidental caprice of the
court, arrest that bore no relation to offence, taxation
inversely proportionate to the ability to pay, these were
the prescriptive privileges that Burke invited his generation to accept as part of the accumulated wisdom of the
past. It is not difficult to see why those who swore their
oath in the tennis-court at Versailles should have felt
such wisdom worthy to be condemned. Burke's caution
was for them the timidity of one who embraces existent
evils rather than fly to the refuge of an accessible good.
In a less degree, the same is true of England. The constitution that Burke called upon men to worship was the
constitution which made the Duke of Bedford powerful,
that gave no representation to Manchester and a member
to Old Sarum, which enacted the game laws and left
upon the statute-book a penal code which hardly yielded
to the noble attack of Romilly. These, which were for
Burke merely the accidental excrescences of a noble
ideal, were for them its inner essence; and where they
could not reform they were willing to destroy.

The revolutionary spirit, in fact, was as much the
product of the past as the very institutions it came to
condemn. The innovations were the inevitable outcome
of past oppression. Burke refused to see that aspect of
the picture. He ascribed to the crime of the present
what was due to the half-wilful errors of the past. The
man who grounded his faith in historic experience
refused to admit as history the elements alien from his
special outlook. He took that liberty not to venerate
where he was unable to comprehend which he denied
to his opponents. Nor did he admit the uses to which
his doctrine of prescription was bound to be put in the

hands of selfish and unscrupulous men. No one will
object to privilege for a Chatham; but privilege for the
Duke of Grafton is a different thing, and Burke's doctrine
safeguards the innumerable men of whom Grafton is
the type in the hope that by happy accident some
Chatham will one day emerge. He justifies the privileges
of the English Church in the name of religious well-
being; but it is difficult to see what men like Watson
or Archbishop Cornwallis have got to do with religion.
The doctrine of prescription might be admirable if all
statesmen were as wise as Burke; but in the hands of
lesser men it becomes no more than the protective
armour of vested interests into the ethics of which it
refuses us leave to examine.

That suspicion of thought is integral to Burke's philosophy, and it deserves more examination than it has
received. In part it is a rejection of the Benthamite
position that man is a reasoning animal. It puts its trust
in habit as the chief source of human action; and it thus
is distrustful of thought as leading into channels to which
the nature of man is not adapted. Novelty, which is
assumed to be the outcome of thought, it regards as
subversive of the routine upon which civilization depends.
Thought is destructive of peace; and it is argued that we
know too little of political phenomena to make us venture
into the untried places to which thought invites us. Yet
the first of many answers is surely the most obvious fact
that if man is so much the creature of his customs, no
reason would prevail save where they proved inadequate.
If thought is simply a reserve power in society, its
strength must obviously depend upon common acceptance; and that can only come when some routine has
failed to satisfy the impulses of men.

But we may urge a difficulty that is even more decisive. No system of habits can ever hope to endure long in a world where the cumulative power of memory enables change to be so swift; and no system of habits can endure at all unless its underlying idea represents the satisfaction of a general desire. It must, that is to say, make rational appeal; and, indeed, as Aristotle said, it can have virtue only to the point where it is conscious of itself. The uncritical routine of which Burke is the sponsor would here deprive the mass of men of virtue. Yet in modern civilization the whole strength of any custom depends upon exactly that consciousness of right which Burke restricted to his aristocracy. Our real need is less the automatic response to ancient stimulus than power to know what stimulus has social value. We need, that is to say, the gift of criticism rather than the gift of inert acceptance. Not, of course, that the habits which Burke so earnestly admired are at all part of our nervous endowment in any integral sense. The short space of the French Revolution made the habit of thinking in terms of progress an essential part of our intellectual inheritance; and where the Burkian school proclaims how exceptional progress has been in history, we take that as proof of the ease with which essential habit may be acquired. Habit, in fact, without philosophy, destroys the finer side of civilized life. It may leave a stratum to whom its riches have been discovered; but it leaves the mass of men soulless automata without spontaneous response to the chords struck by another hand.

Burke's answer would, of course, have been that he was not a democrat. He did not trust the people and he rated their capacity as low. He thought of the people —it was obviously a generalization from his time—as consistently prone to disorder and checked only by the force of ancient habit. Yet he has himself supplied the answer to that attitude. ' My observation ', he said in his *Speech on the East India Bill*, ' has furnished me with nothing that is to be found in any habits of life or education which tends wholly to disqualify men for the functions of government.' We can go further than that sober caution. We know that there is one technique only capable of securing good government and that is the training of the mass of men to interest in it. We know that no State can hope for peace in which large types of experience are without representation. Indeed, if proof were here wanting, an examination of the eighteenth century would supply it. Few would deny that statesmen are capable of disinterested sacrifice for classes of whose inner life they are ignorant; yet the relation between law and the interest of the dominant class is too intimate to permit with safety the exclusion of a part of the State from sharing in its guidance. Nor did Burke remember his own wise saying that ' in all disputes between the people and their rulers the presumption is at least upon a par in favour of the people '; and he quotes with agreement that great sentence of Sully's which traces popular violence to popular suffering. No one can watch the economic struggles of the eighteenth and nineteenth centuries or calculate the pain they have involved to humble men, without admitting that they represent the final protest of an outraged mind against oppression too intolerable to be borne. Burke himself, as his own speeches show, knew little or nothing of the pain involved in the agrarian changes of his age. The one way to avoid violent outbreak is not exclusion of the people from power but their participation in it. The popular sense of right may often, as Aristotle saw, be wiser than the opinion of statesmen. It is not necessary to equate the worth of untrained common sense with experienced wisdom to suggest that, in the long run, neglect of common sense will make the effort of that wisdom fruitless.

This, indeed, is to take the lowest ground. For the case against Burke's aristocracy has a moral aspect with which he did not deal. He did not inquire by what right a handful of men were to be hereditary governors of a whole people. Expediency is no answer to the question, for Bentham was presently to show how shallow was that basis of consent. Once it is admitted that the personality of men is entitled to respect, institutional room must be found for its expression. The State is morally stunted where their powers go undeveloped. There is something curious here in Burke's inability to suspect deformity in a system which gave his talents but partial place. He must have known that no one in the House of Commons was his equal. He must have known how few of those he called upon to recognize the splendour of their function were capable of playing the part he pictured for them. The answer to a morally bankrupt aristocracy is surely not the overwhelming effort required in its purification when the plaintiff is the people; for the mere fact that the people is the plaintiff is already evidence of its fitness for power. Burke gave no hint of how the level of his governing class could be maintained. He said nothing of what education might accomplish for the people. He did not examine the obvious consequences of their economic status. Had his eyes not been obscured by passion, the work of that States-General, the names in which appeared to him so astonishing in their inexperience, might have given him pause. The 'obscure provincial advocates . . . stewards of petty local jurisdictions . . . the fomenters and conductors of the petty war of village vexation' legislated, out of their inexperience, for the world. Their resolution, their constancy, their high sense of the national need, were precisely the qualities Burke demanded in his governing class; and the States-General did not move from the straight path he laid down until they met with intrigue from those of whom Burke became the licensed champion.

Nor is it in the least clear that his emphasis upon expediency is, in any real way, a release from metaphysical inquiry. Rather may it be urged that what was needed in Burke's philosophy was the clear avowal of the metaphysic it implied. Nothing is more greatly wanted in political inquiry than discovery of that 'intuition more subtle than any articulate major premise', which, as Justice Holmes has said, is the true foundation of so many of our political judgements. The theory of natural rights upon which Burke heaped such contempt was wrong rather in its form than in its substance. It clearly suffered from its mistaken effort to trace to an imaginary state of nature what was due to a complex experience. It suffered also from its desire to lay down universal formulae. It needed to state the rights demanded in terms of the social interests they involved rather than in the abstract ethic they implied. But the demands which underlay the thought of men like Price and Priestley was as much the offspring of experience as Burke's own doctrine. They made, indeed, the tactical mistake of seeking to give an unripe philosophic form to a political strategy wherein, clearly enough, Burke was their master. But no one can read the answers of

Paine and Mackintosh, who both were careful to avoid the panoply of metaphysics, to the *Reflections*, without feeling that Burke failed to move them from their main position. Expediency may be admirable in telling the statesman what to do; but it does not explain the sources of his ultimate act, nor justify the thing finally done. The unconscious deeps which lie beneath the surface of the mind are rarely less urgent than the motives that are avowed. Action is less their elimination than their index; and we must penetrate within their recesses before we have the full materials for judgement.

Considered in this fashion, the case for natural rights is surely unanswerable. The things that men desire correspond, in some rough fashion, to the things they need. Natural rights are nothing more than the armour evolved to protect their vital interests. Upon the narrow basis of legal history it is, of course, impossible to protect them. History is rather the record of the thwarting of human desire than of its achievement. But upon the value of certain things there is a sufficient and constant opinion to give us assurance that repression will ultimately involve disorder. Nor is there any difference between the classes of men in this regard. Forms, indeed, will vary; and the power we have of answering demand will always wait upon the discoveries of science. Our natural rights, that is to say, will have a changing content simply because this is not a static world. But that does not mean, as Burke insisted, that they are empty of experience. They come, of course, mainly from men who have been excluded from intimate contact with the fruits of power. Nonconformists in religion, workers without land or capital save the power of their own hands, they draw, as demands, their strength from the disinherited.

M

Yet it is difficult to see, as Burke would undoubtedly have insisted, that they are the worse from the source whence they derive. Rather do they point to grave inadequacy in the substance of the State, inadequacy neglect of which has led to the cataclysms of historic experience. The unwillingness of Burke to examine into their foundation reveals his lack of moral insight into the problem he confronted.

That lack of insight must, of course, be given some explanation; and its cause seems rooted in Burke's metaphysic outlook. He was profoundly religious; and he did not doubt that the order of the universe was the command of God. It was, as a consequence, beneficent; and to deny its validity was, for him, to doubt the wisdom of God. 'Having disposed', he wrote, 'and marshalled us by a divine tactic, not according to our will, but to His, He had, in and by that disposition, vitally subjected us to act the part which belongs to the place assigned us.' The State, in fact, is to be built upon the sacrifice of men; and this they must accept as of the will of God. We are to do our duty in our allotted station without repining, in anticipation, doubtless, of a later reward. What we are is thus the expression of his goodness; and there is a real sense in which Burke may be said to have maintained the inherent rightness of the existing order. Certainly he throws a cloak of religious veneration about the purely metaphysical concept of property; and his insistence upon the value of peace as opposed to truth is surely part of the same attitude. Nor is it erroneous to connect this background with his antagonism to the French Revolution. What was most distressing to him was the overthrowing of the Church, and he did not hesitate, in

very striking fashion, to connect revolutionary opinion
with infidelity. Indeed Burke, like Locke, seems to have
been convinced that a social sense was impossible in an
atheist; and his *Letters on a Regicide Peace* have a good
deal of that relentless illogic which made de Maistre
connect the first sign of dissent from ultramontanism
with the road to a denial of all faith. Nothing is more
difficult than to deal with a thinker who has had a
revelation; and this sense that the universe was a divine
mystery not to be too nearly scrutinized by man grew
greatly upon Burke in his later years. It was not an
attitude which reason could overthrow; for its first
principle was an awe in the presence of facts to which
reason is a stranger.

There is, moreover, in Burke a Platonic idealism
which made him, like later thinkers of the school, regard
existing difficulties with something akin to complacent
benevolence. What interested him was the idea of the
English State; and whatever, as he thought, deformed
it, was not of the essence of its nature. He denied, that
is to say, that the degree to which a purpose is fulfilled
is as important as the purpose itself. A thing becomes
good by the end it has in view; and the deformities of
time and place ought not to lead us to deny the beauty
of the end. It is the great defect of all idealistic philosophy that it should come to the examination of facts
in so optimistic a temper. It never sufficiently realizes
that in the transition from theoretic purpose to practical
realization a significant transformation may occur. We
do not come to grips with the facts. What we are bidden
to remember is the splendour of what the facts are trying
to be. The existing order is beatified as a necessary stage
in a beneficent process. We are not to separate out the

constituent elements therein, and judge them as facts
in time and space. Society is one and indivisible; and
the defects do not at any point impair the ultimate
integrity of the social bond.

Yet it is surely evident that in the heat and stress of
social life, we cannot afford so long a period as the
basis for our judgement. We may well enough regard
the corruption of the monarchy under the later Hanoverians as the necessary prelude to its purification under
Victoria; but that does not make it any the less corrupt.
We may even see how a monistic view of society is
possible to one who, like Burke, is uniquely occupied
with the public good. But the men who, like Muir and
Hardy in the treason trials of the Revolution, think
rather in terms of the existing disharmonies than the
beauty of the purpose upon which they rest, are only
human if they think those disharmonies more real than
the purpose they do not meet. They were surely to be
pardoned if, reading the *Reflections* of Burke, they regarded class distinctions as more vital than their harmony of interest, when they saw the tenacity with which
privileges they did not share were defended. It is even
possible to understand why some insisted that if those
privileges were, as Burke had argued, essential to the
construction of the whole, it was against that whole,
alike in purpose and in realization, that they were in
revolt. For them the fact of discontinuity was vital.
They could not but ask for happiness in their own individual lives no less than in the State of which they
were part. They came to see that without self-government in the sense of their own active participation in
power, such happiness must go unfulfilled. The State,
in fact, may have the noblest purpose; but its object is

attempted by agents who are also mortal men. The
basis of their scrutiny became at once pragmatic. The
test of allegiance to established institutions became immediately the achievement for which they were responsible. The achievement, as they urged, was hardly
written with adequacy in terms of the lives of humble
men. That was why they judged no attitude of worth
which sought the equation of the real and the ideal.
The first lesson of their own experience of power was
the need for its limitation by the instructed judgement
of free minds.[1]

## VI

No man was more deeply hostile to the early politics
of the romantic movement, to the *Contrat Social* of
Rousseau and the *Political Justice* of Godwin, than was
Burke; yet, on the whole, it is with the romantics that
Burke's fundamental influence remains. His attitude to
reason, his exaltation of passion and imagination over
the conscious logic of men, were of the inmost stuff of
which they were made. In that sense, at least, his kinship is with the great conservative revolution of the
generation which followed him. Hegel and Savigny in
Germany, de Maistre and Bonald in France, Coleridge
and the later Wordsworth in England, are in a true
sense his disciples. That does not mean that any of them
were directly conscious of his work, but that the movement he directed had its necessary outcome in their
defence of his ideals. The path of history is strewn with
undistributed middles; and it is possible that in the
clash between his attitude and that of Bentham there

[1] Cf. my *Authority in the Modern State*, pp. 65–9.

were the materials for a fuller synthesis in a later time. Certainly there is no more admirable corrective in historical politics than the contrast they afford.

It is easy to praise Burke and easier still to miss the greatness of his effort. Perspective apart, he is destined doubtless to live rather as the author of some maxims that few statesmen will dare to forget than as the creator of a system which, even in its unfinished implications, is hardly less gigantic than that of Hobbes or Bentham. His very defects are lessons in themselves. His unhesitating inability to see how dangerous is the concentration of property is standing proof that men are over-prone to judge the rightness of a State by their own wishes. His own contempt for the results of reasonable inquiry is a ceaseless lesson in the virtue of consistent scrutiny of our inheritance. His disregard of popular desire suggests the fatal ease with which we neglect the opinion of those who stand outside the active centre of political conflict. Above all, his hostility to the Revolution should at least make later generations beware lest novelty of outlook be unduly confounded with erroneous doctrine.

Yet even when such deduction has been made, there is hardly a greater figure in the history of political thought in England. Without the relentless logic of Hobbes, the acuteness of Hume, the moral insight of T. H. Green, he has a large part of the faculties of each. He brought to the political philosophy of his generation a sense of its direction, a lofty vigour of purpose, and a full knowledge of its complexity, such as no other statesman has ever possessed. His flashes of insight are things that go, as few men have ever gone, into the hidden deeps of political complexity. Unquestionably, his speculation is rather that of the orator in the tribune than of the thinker in his study. He never forgot his party, and he wrote always in that House of Commons atmosphere which makes a man unjust to the argument and motives of his opponent. Yet, when the last word of criticism has been made, the balance of illumination is immense. He illustrates at its best the value of that party-system the worth of which made so deep an impression on all he wrote. He showed that government by discussion can be made to illuminate great principles. He showed also that allegiance to party is never inconsistent with the deeper allegiance to the demand of conscience. When he came to the House of Commons, the prospects of representative government were very dark; and it is mainly to his emphasis upon its virtues that its victory must be attributed. Institutional change is likely to be more rapid than in his generation; for we seem to have reached that moment when, as he foresaw, 'they who persist in opposing that mighty current will appear rather to resist the decrees of Providence itself than the mere designs of men'. The principles upon which we proceed are doubtless different from those that he commended; yet his very challenge to their wisdom only gives to his warning a deeper inspiration for our effort.

## CHAPTER VII

# THE FOUNDATIONS OF ECONOMIC LIBERALISM

## I

THE Industrial Revolution is hardly less a fundamental change in the habits of English thought than in the technique of commercial production. Alongside the discoveries of Hargreaves and Crompton, the ideas of Hume and Adam Smith shifted the whole perspective of men's minds. The Revolution, indeed, like all great movements, did not originate at any given moment. There was no sudden invention which made the hampering system of government-control seem incompatible with industrial advance. The mercantilism against which the work of Adam Smith was so magistral a protest was already rather a matter of external than internal commerce when he wrote. He triumphed less because he suddenly opened men's eyes to a truth hitherto concealed than because he represented the culmination of certain principles which, under various aspects, were common to his time. The movement for religious toleration is not only paralleled in the next century by the movement for economic freedom, but is itself in a real sense the parent of the latter. For it is not without significance that the pre-Adamite economists were almost without exception the urgent defenders of religious toleration. The landowners were churchmen, the men

of commerce largely Nonconformist; and religious proscription interfered with the balance of trade. When the
roots of religious freedom had been secured, it was easy
for them to transfer their argument to the secular sphere.

Nothing, indeed, is more important in the history of
English political philosophy than to realize that from
Stuart times the Nonconformists were deeply bitten with
distrust of government. Its courts of special instance
hampered industrial life at every turn in the interest of
religious conformity. Their heavy fines and irritating
restrictions upon foreign workmen were nothing so much
as a tax upon industrial progress. What the Nonconformists wanted was to be left alone; and Davenant
explained the root of their desire when he tells of the
gaols crowded with substantial tradesmen whose im-
prisonment spelt unemployment for thousands of workmen. Sir William Temple, in his description of Holland,
represents economic prosperity as the child of toleration.
The movement for ecclesiastical freedom in England,
moreover, became casually linked with that protest
against the system of monopolies with which it was the
habit of the court to reward its favourites. Freedom in
economic matters, like freedom in religion, came rapidly
to mean permission that diversity shall exist; and
economic diversity soon came to mean free competition.
The latter easily became imbued with religious significance. English puritanism, as Troeltsch has shown us,
insisted that work was the will of God and its performance the test of grace. The greater the energy of its
performance, the greater the likelihood of prosperity;
and thence it is but a step to argue that the free development of a man's industrial worth is the law of God.
Success in business, indeed, became for many a test of

religious grace, and poverty the proof of God's disfavour. Books like Steele's *Religious Tradesman* (1684) show clearly how close is the connexion. The hostility of the English landowners to the commercial classes in the eighteenth century is at bottom the inheritance of religious antagonism. The typical qualities of dissent became a certain pushful exertion by which the external criteria of salvation could be secured.

Much of the contemporary philosophy, moreover, fits in with this attitude. From the time of Bacon, the main object of speculation was to disrupt the scholastic teleology. In the result the State becomes dissolved into a discrete mass of individuals, and the self-interest of each is the starting-point of all inquiry. Hobbes built his State upon the selfishness of men; even Locke makes the individual enter political life for the benefits that accrue therefrom. The cynicism of Mandeville, the utilitarianism of Hume, are only by-paths of the same tradition. The organic society of the Middle Ages gives place to an individual who builds the State out of his own desires. Liberty becomes their realization; and the object of the State is to enable men in the fullest sense to secure the satisfaction of their private wants. How far is that conception from the Anglican outlook of the seventeenth century, a sermon of Laud's makes clear. ' If any man ', he said,[1] ' be so addicted to his private interest that he neglects the common State, he is void of the sense of piety, and wishes peace and happiness for himself in vain. For, whoever he be, he must live in the body of the commonwealth and in the body of the Church.' So Platonic an outlook was utterly alien from the temper of puritanism. They had no thought of

[1] Sermon of 19 June 1621. *Works* (ed. of 1847), p. 28.

sacrificing themselves to an institution which they had much ground for thinking existed only for their torment. The development of the religious instinct to the level of salvation found its philosophic analogue in the development of the economic sense of fitness. The State became the servant of the individual from being his master; and service became equated with an internal policy of *laissez-faire*.

Such summary, indeed, abridges the long process of release from which the eighteenth century had still to suffer; nor does it sufficiently insist upon the degree to which the old idea of State control still held sway in external policies of trade. Mercantilism was still in the ascendant when Adam Smith came to write. Few statesmen of importance before the younger Pitt had learned the secret of its fallacies; and, indeed, the chief ground for difference between Chatham and Burke was the former's suspicion that Burke had embraced the noxious doctrine of free trade. Mercantilism, by the time of Locke, is not the simple error that wealth consists in bullion but the insistence that the balance of trade must be preserved. Partly it was doubtless derived from the methods of the old political arithmetic of men like Petty and Davenant; the individual seeks a balance at the end of his year's accounting and so, too, the State must have a balance. ' A Kingdom ', said Locke, ' grows rich or poor just as a farmer does, and no other way '; and while there is a sense in which this is wholly true, the meaning attached to it by the mercantilists was that foreign competition meant national weakness. They could not conceive a commercial bargain which was profitable to both sides. Nations grow prosperous at each other's expense; wherefore a woollen trade in

Ireland necessarily spells English unemployment. Even Davenant, who was in many respects on the high road to free trade, was in this problem adamant. Protection was essential in the colonial market; for unless the trade of the colonies was directed through England they might be dangerous rivals. So Ireland and America were sacrificed to the fear of British merchants, with the inevitable result that repression brought from both the obvious search for remedy.

Herein it might appear that Adam Smith had novelty to contribute; yet nothing is more certain than that his full sense of the world as the only true unit of marketing was fully grasped before him. In 1691 Sir Dudley North published his *Discourses upon Trade*. Therein he clearly sees that commercial barriers between Great Britain and France are basically as senseless as would be commercial barriers between Yorkshire and Middlesex. Indeed, in one sense, North goes even further than Adam Smith, for he argues against the usury laws in terms Bentham would hardly have disowned. Ten years later an anonymous writer in a tract entitled *Considerations on the East India Trade* (1701) has no illusions about the evil of monopoly. He sees with striking clarity that the real problem is not at any cost to maintain the industries a nation actually possesses, but to have the national capital applied in the most efficient channels. So, too, Hume dismissed the mercantile theory with the contemptuous remark that it was trying to keep water beyond its proper level. Tucker, as has been pointed out, was a free-trader, and his opinion of the American war was that it was as mad as those who fought ' under the peaceful Cross to recover the Holy Land '; and he urged, indeed prophesied, the union with Ireland in the

interest of commercial amity. Nor must the emphasis
of the Physiocrats upon free trade be forgotten. There
is no evidence now that Adam Smith owed this perception to his acquaintance with Quesnay and Turgot;
but they may well have confirmed him in it, and they
show that the older philosophy was attacked on every
side.

Nor must we miss the general atmosphere of the time.
On the whole his age was a conservative one, convinced,
without due reason, that happiness was independent of
birth or wealth and that natural law somehow could
be made to justify existing institutions. The poets, like
Pope, were singing of the small part of life which kings
and laws may hope to cure; and that attitude is written
in the general absence of economic legislation during the
period. Religiously, the Church exalted the *status quo*;
and where, as with Wesley, there was revolt, its impetus
directed the mind to the source of salvation in the
individual act. It may, indeed, be generally argued that
the religious teachers acted as a social soporific. Where
riches accumulated, they could be regarded as the
blessing of God; where they were absent their un-
importance for eternal happiness could be emphasized.
Burke's early attack on a system which condemned ' two
hundred thousand innocent persons . . . to so intolerable
slavery ' was, in truth, a justification of the existing
order. The social question which, in the previous century,
men like Bellers and Winstanley had brought into view,
dropped out of notice until the last quarter of the
century. There was, that is to say, no organized resistance
possible to the power of individualism; and resistance
was unlikely to make itself heard once the resources of
the Industrial Revolution were brought into play. Men

discovered with something akin to ecstasy the possibilities of the new inventions; and when the protest
came against the misery they effected, it was answered
that they represented the working of that natural law
by which the energies of men may raise them to success.
And discontent could easily, as with the saintly Wilberforce, be countered by the assertion that it was revolt
against the will of God.

## II

Few lives represent more splendidly than that of
Adam Smith the speculative ideal of a dispassionate
study of philosophy. He was fortunate in his teachers
and his friends. At Glasgow he was the pupil of Francis
Hutcheson; and even if he was taught nothing at
Oxford, at least six years of leisure gave him ample
opportunity to learn. His professorship at Glasgow not
only brought him into contact with men like Hume,
but also admitted him to intercourse with a group of
business men whose liberal sentiments on commerce
undoubtedly strengthened, if they did not originate, his
own liberal views. At Glasgow, too, in 1759, he published his *Theory of Moral Sentiments*, written with sufficient
power of style to obscure its inner poverty of thought.
The book brought him immediately a distinguished
reputation from a public which exalted elegance of
diction beyond all literary virtues. The volatile Charles
Townshend made him tutor to the Duke of Buccleuch,
through whom Smith not only secured comparative
affluence for the rest of his days, but also a French tour
in which he met at its best the most brilliant society in
Europe. The germ of his *Wealth of Nations* already lay

hidden in those Glasgow lectures which Edwin Cannan
so happily recovered for us; and it was in a moment of
leisure in France that he set to work to put them together in systematic fashion. Not, indeed, that the
Frenchmen whom he met, Turgot, Quesnay, and Du-
pont de Nemours, can be said to have done more than
confirm the truths he had already been teaching. When
he returned to Scotland and a competence, ten years
of constant labour were necessary before *The Wealth of
Nations* was complete. After its publication, in 1776,
Adam Smith did little save attend to the administrative
duties of a minor, but lucrative office in the Customs.
Until the end, indeed, he never quite gave up the hope,
foreshadowed first in the *Moral Sentiments*, of completing
a gigantic survey of civilized institutions. But he was a
slow worker, and his health was never robust. It was
enough that he should have written his book and
cherished friendships such as it is given to few men to
possess. Hume and Burke, Millar the jurist, James
Watt, Foulis the printer, Black the chemist, and Hutton
of geological fame—it is an enviable circle. He had
known Turgot on intimate terms and visited Voltaire
on Lake Geneva. Hume had told him that his book
had ' depth and solidity and acuteness '; the younger
Pitt had consulted him on public affairs. Few men have
moved amid such happy peace within the very centre
of what was most illustrious in their age.

We are less concerned here with the specific economic
details of *The Wealth of Nations* than with its general
attitude to the State. But here a limitation upon criticism
must be noted. The man of whom Smith writes is man
in search of wealth; by definition the economic motive
dominates his actions. Such abuse, therefore, as Ruskin

poured upon him is really beside the point when his
objective is borne in mind. What virtually he does is to
assume the existence of a natural economic order which
tends, when unrestrained by counter-tendencies, to
secure the happiness of men. 'That order of things
which necessity imposes in general,' he writes, '. . . is,
in every particular country promoted by the natural
inclinations of man'; and he goes on to explain what
would have resulted 'if human institutions had never
thwarted those natural inclinations'. 'All systems either
of preference or of restraint, therefore, being thus completely taken away,' he writes again, 'the obvious and
simple system of natural liberty establishes itself of its
own accord. Every man, as long as he does not violate
the laws of justice, is left perfectly free to pursue his
own interest in his own way. . . . The sovereign is completely discharged from a duty in the attempting to
perform which he must always be exposed to innumerable
delusions, and for the proper performance of which no
human wisdom or knowledge would ever be sufficient;
the duty of superintending the industry of private people
and of directing it towards the employments most
suitable to the interests of the society.'

The State, in this conception, has but three functions
—defence, justice, and 'the duty of erecting and main-
taining certain public works and certain public institutions which it can never be for the interest of any individual, or small number of individuals, to erect and
maintain'. The State, in fact, is simply to provide the
atmosphere in which production is possible. Nor does
Smith conceal his thought that the main function of
justice is the protection of property. 'The affluence of
the rich', he wrote, 'excites the indignation of the poor,

who are often both driven by want and prompted by
envy to invade their possessions. It is only under the
shelter of the civil magistrate that the owner of that
valuable property, acquired by the labour of many
years, or perhaps many successive generations, can sleep
a single night in security.' The attitude, indeed, is in-
tensified by his constant sense that the capital which
makes possible new productivity is the outcome of men's
sacrifice; to protect it is thus to safeguard the sources
of wealth itself. And even if the State is entrusted with
education and the prevention of disease, this is rather
for the general benefit they confer and the doubt that
private enterprise would find them profitable than as
the expression of a general rule. Collective effort of every
kind awakened in him a deep distrust. Trade regulations
such as the limitation of apprenticeship he condemned
as ' manifest encroachment upon the just liberty of the
workman and of those who may be disposed to employ
him '. Even educational establishments are suspect on
the ground—not unnatural after his own experience of
Oxford—that their possibilities of comfort may enervate
the natural energies of men.

The key to this attitude is clear enough. The improvement of society is due, he thinks, not to the calculations
of government but to the natural instincts of economic
man. We cannot avoid the impulse to better our condition; and the less its effort is restrained the more
certain it is that happiness will result. We gain, in fact,
some sense of its inherent power when we bear in mind
the magnitude of its accomplishment despite the folly
and extravagance of princes. Therein we have some
index of what it would achieve if left unhindered to
work out its own destinies. Human institutions con-

N

tinually thwart its power; for those who build those
institutions are moved rather ' by the momentary fluc-
tuations of affairs ' than their true nature. ' That insidious and crafty animal, vulgarly called a politician
or statesman ' meets little mercy for his effort compared
to the magic power of the natural order. ' In all countries
where there is a tolerable security,' he writes, ' every
man of common understanding will endeavour to employ
whatever stock he can command in procuring either
present enjoyment or future profit.' Individual spontaneity is thus the root of economic good; and the real
justification of the State is the protection it affords to
this impulse. Man, in fact, is by nature a trader and
he is bound by nature to discover the means most apt
to progress.

Nor was he greatly troubled by differences of fortune.
Like most of the Scottish school, especially Hutcheson
and Hume, he thought that men are much alike in
happiness, whatever their station or endowments. For
there is a ' never-failing certainty ' that ' all men sooner
or later accommodate themselves to whatever becomes
their permanent situation '; though he admits that there
is a certain level below which poverty and misery go
hand in hand. But, for the most part, happiness is
simply a state of mind; and he seems to have had but
little suspicion that differences of wealth might issue in
dangerous social consequence. Men, moreover, he regarded as largely equal in their original powers; and
differences of character he ascribes to the various occu-
pations implied in the division of labour. Each man,
therefore, as he follows his self-interest, promotes the
general happiness of society. That principle is inherent
in the social order. ' Every man ', he wrote in the *Moral*

*Sentiments,* ' is by nature first and principally recommended to his own care ' and therein he is ' led by an invisible hand to promote an end which was no part of his intention '. The State, that is to say, is the sum of individual goods; whereby to better ourselves is clearly to its benefit. And that desire ' which comes with us from the womb and never leaves us till we go to the grave ' is the more efficacious the less it is restrained by governmental artifice. For we know so well what makes us happy that none can hope to help us so much as we help ourselves.

Enlightened selfishness is thus the root of prosperity; but we must not fall into the easy fallacy which makes Smith deaf to the plaint of the poor. He urged the employer to have regard to the health and welfare of the worker, a regard which was the voice of reason and humanity. Where there was conflict between love of the *status quo* and a social good which revolution alone could achieve, he did not, at least in the *Moral Sentiments,* hesitate to choose the latter. Order was, for the most part, indispensable; but ' the greatest and noblest of all characters ' he made the reformer of the State. Yet he is too impressed by the working of natural economic laws to belittle their influence. Employers, in his picture, are little capable of benevolence or charity. Their rule is the law of supply and demand and not the Sermon on the Mount. They combine without hesitation to depress wages to the lowest point of subsistence. They seize every occasion of commercial misfortune to make better terms for themselves; and the greater the poverty the more submissive do servants become so that scarcity is naturally regarded as more favourable to industry.

Obviously enough, the inner hinge of all this argument is Smith's conception of nature. Nor can there be much doubt of what he thought its inner substance. Facile distinctions such as the effort of Buckle to show that while in the *Moral Sentiments* Adam Smith was dealing with the unselfish side of man's nature, in *The Wealth of Nations* he was dealing with a group of facts which required the abstraction of such altruistic elements, are really beside the point. Nature for Smith is simply the spontaneous action of human character unchecked by hindrances of State. It is, as Bonar has aptly said, ' a vindication of the unconscious law present in the separate actions of men when these actions are directed by a certain strong personal motive '. Adam Smith's argument is an assumption that the facts can be made to show the relative powerlessness of institutions in the face of economic laws grounded in human psychology. The psychology itself is relatively simple, and, at least in *The Wealth of Nations*, not greatly different from the avowed assumptions of utilitarianism. He emphasizes the strength of reason in the economic field, and his sense that it enables men to judge much better of their best interests than an external authority can hope to do. And therefore the practices accomplished by this reason are those in which the impulses of men are to be found. The order they represent is the natural order; and whatever hinders its full operation is an unwise check upon the things for which men strive.

Obviously enough, this attitude runs the grave risk of seeming to abstract a single motive—the desire for wealth—from the confused welter of human impulses and to make it dominant at the expense of human nature itself. A hasty reading of Adam Smith would, indeed, confirm that impression; and that is perhaps why he seemed to Ruskin to blaspheme human nature. But a more careful survey, particularly when the *Moral Sentiments* is borne in mind, suggests a different conclusion. His attitude is implicit in the general medium in which he worked. What he was trying to do was less to emphasize that men care above all things for the pursuit of wealth than that no institutional modifications are able to destroy the power of that motive to labour. There is too much history in *The Wealth of Nations* to make tenable the hypothesis of complete abstraction. And there is, even, a clear sense of a nature behind his custom when he speaks of a 'sacred regard' for life, and urges that every man has property in his own labour. The truth here surely is that Smith was living in a time of commercial expansion. What was evident to him was the potential wealth to be made available if the obsolete system of restraint could be destroyed. Liberty to him meant absence of restraint not because its more positive aspect was concealed from him but rather because the kind of freedom wanted in the environment in which he moved was exactly that for which he made his plea. There is a hint that freedom as a positive thing was known to him from the fact that he relied upon education to relieve the evils of the division of labour. But the general context of his book required less emphasis upon the virtues of State interference than upon its defects. His cue was to show that all the benefits of regulation had been achieved despite its interference; from which, of course, it followed that restraint was a matter of supererogation.

## III

It would be tedious to praise *The Wealth of Nations*. It may be doubtful whether Buckle's ecstatic judgement that it has had more influence than any other book in the world was justified even when he wrote; but certainly it is one of the seminal books of the modern time. What is more important is to note the perspective in which its main teaching was set. He wrote in the midst of the first significant beginnings of the Industrial Revolution; and his emphatic approval of Watt's experiments suggests that he was not unalive to its importance. Yet it cannot in any full sense be said that the Industrial Revolution has a large part in his book. The picture of industrial organization and its possibilities is too simple to suggest that he had caught any far-reaching glimpse into the future. Industry, for him, is still in the last stage of handicraft; it is a matter of skilful workmanship and not of mechanical appliance. Capital is still the laborious result of parsimony. Credit is spoken of rather in the tones of one who sees it less as a new instrument of finance than a dangerous attempt by the aspiring needy to scale the heights of wealth. Profits are always a justified return for productive labour; interest the payment for the use of the owner's past parsimony. Business is still the middleman distributing to the consumer on a small scale. He did not, or could not, conceive of any industry either so vast or so depersonalized as at present. He was rather writing of a system which, like the politics of the eighteenth century, had reached an equilibrium of passable comfort. His natural order was, at bottom, the beatification of that to which this equilibrium tended. Its benefits might be improved by free trade and free workmanship; but, upon the whole, he saw no reason to call in question its fundamental dogmas.

Therein, of course, may be found the main secret of his omissions. The problem of labour finds no place in his book. The things that the poor have absent from their lives, that concept of a national minimum below which no State can hope to fulfil even the meanest of its aims, of these he has no conception. Rather the note of the book is a quiet optimism, impressed by the possibilities of constant improvement which lie embedded in the human impulse to better itself. What he did not see is the way in which the logical outcome of the system he describes may well be the attainment of great wealth at a price in human cost that is beyond its worth. Therein, it is clear, all individualistic theories of the State miss the true essence of the social bond. Those who came after Adam Smith saw only half his problem. He wrote a consumer's theory of value. But whereas he had in mind a happy and contented people, the economics of Ricardo and Malthus seized upon a single element in human nature as that which alone the State must serve. Freedom from restraint came ultimately to mean a judgement upon national well-being in terms of the volume of trade. 'It is not with happiness,' said Nassau Senior, 'but with wealth that I am concerned as a political economist; and I am not only justified in omitting, but am perhaps bound to omit, all considerations which have no influence upon wealth.'

In such an aspect, it was natural for the balance of investigation to swing towards the study of the technique of production; and with the growing importance of capital, as machinery was introduced, the worker, without difficulty, became an adjunct, easily replaced, to the machine. What was remembered then was the side of Adam Smith which looked upon enlightened selfishness as the key to social good. Regulation became anathema even when the evils it attempted to restrain were those which made the mass of the people incapable of citizenship. Even national education was regarded as likely to destroy initiative; or, as a pauper's dole which men of self-respect would regard with due abhorrence. The State, in short, ceased to concern itself with justice save in so far as the administration of a judicial code spelled the protection of the new industrial system. Nothing is more striking in the half-century after Adam Smith than the optimism of the economist and the business man in contrast to the hopeless despair of labour. That men can organize to improve their lot was denied with emphasis, so that until Francis Place even the workers themselves were half-convinced. The manufacturers were the State; and the whole intellectual strength of economics was massed to prove the rightness of the equation. The literature of protest, men like Hall and Thompson, Hodgskin and Bray, exerted no influence upon the legislation of the time; and Robert Owen was deemed an amiable eccentric rather than the prophet of a new hope. The men who succeeded, as Wilberforce, carried out to the letter the unstated assumptions of Puritan economics. The poor were consigned to a God whose dictates were by definition beneficent; and if they failed to understand the curious incidence of his rewards that was because his ways were inscrutable. No one who reads the tracts of writers like Harriet Martineau can fail to see how pitiless was the operation of this attitude. Life is made a struggle, beneficent indeed, but deriving its ultimate meaning from the misery incident to it. The tragedy is excused because the export trade increases in its volume. The iron law of wages, the assumed transition of every energetic worker to the ranks of wealth, the danger lest the natural ability of the worker to better his condition be sapped by giving to him that which his self-respect can better win—these became the unconscious assumptions of all economic discussion.

In all this, as in the foundation with which Adam Smith provided it, we must not miss the element of truth that it contains. No poison is more subtly destructive of the democratic State than paternalism; and the release of the creative impulses of men must always be the coping-stone of public policy. Adam Smith is the supreme representative of a tradition which saw that release effected by individual effort. Where each man cautiously pursued the good as he saw it, the realization was bound, in his view, to be splendid. A population each element of which was active and alert to its economic problems could not escape the achievement of greatness. All that is true; but it evades the obvious conditions we have inherited. For even when the psychological inadequacies of Smith's attitude are put aside, we can judge his theory in the light of the experience it summarizes. Once it is admitted that the object of the State is the achievement of the good life, the final canon of politics is bound to be a moral one. We have to inquire into the dominant conception of the good life, the number of those upon whom it is intended that good shall be conferred.

In the light of this conception it is obvious enough

that Smith's view is impossible. No mere conflict of private interests, however pure in motive, seems able to achieve a harmony of interest between the members of the State. Liberty, in the sense of a positive and equal opportunity for self-realization, is impossible save upon the basis of the acceptance of certain minimal standards which can get accepted only through collective effort. Smith did not see that in the processes of politics what gets accepted is not the will that is at every moment a part of the State purpose, but the will of those who in fact operate the machinery of government. In the half-century after he wrote the men who dominated political life were, with the best intentions, moved by motives at most points unrelated to the national well-being. The fellow-servant doctrine would never have obtained acceptance in a State where, as he thought, employer and workman stood upon an equal footing. Opposition to the Factory Acts would never have developed in a community where it was realized that below certain standards of subsistence the very concept of humanity is impossible. Modern achievement implies a training in the tools of life; and that, for most, is denied even in our own day to the vast majority of men. In the absence of legislation, it is certain that those who employ the services of men will be their political masters; and it will follow that their Acts of Parliament will be adapted to the needs of property. That shrinkage of the purpose of the State will mean for most not merely hardship but degradation of all that makes life worthy. Upon those stunted existences, indeed, a wealthy civilization may easily be builded. Yet it will be a civilization of slaves rather than of men.

The individualism, that is to say, for which Adam

Smith was zealous demands a different institutional expression from that which he gave it. We must not assume an *a priori* justification for the forces of the past. The customs of men may represent the thwarting of the impulses of the many at the expense of the few not less easily than they may embody a general desire; and it is surely a mistaken usage to dignify as natural whatever may happen to have occurred. A man may find self-realization not less in working for the common good than in the limited satisfaction of his narrow desire for material advancement. And that, indeed, is the starting-point of modern effort. Our liberty means the consistent expression of our personality in media where we find people like-minded with ourselves in their conception of social life. The very scale of civilization implies collective plans and common effort. The constant revision of our basic notions was inevitable immediately science was applied to industry. There was thus no reason to believe that the system of individual interests for which Smith stood sponsor was more likely to fit requirements of a new time than one which implied the national regulation of business enterprise. The danger in every period of history is lest we take our own age as the term in institutional evolution. Private enterprise has the sanction of prescription; but since the Industrial Revolution the chief lesson we have had to learn is the unsatisfactory character of that title. History is an unenviable record of bad metaphysics used to defend obsolete systems. It took almost a century after the publication of *The Wealth of Nations* for men to realize that its axioms represented the experience of a definite time. Smith thought of freedom in the terms most suitable to his generation and stated them with a largeness of view which remains impressive even at a century's distance.

But nothing is more certain in the history of political philosophy than that the problem of freedom changes with each age. The nineteenth century sought release from political privilege; and it built its success upon the system prepared by its predecessor. It can never be too greatly emphasized that in each age the substance of liberty will be found in what the dominating forces of that age most greatly want. With Locke, with Smith, with Hegel, and with Marx, the ultimate hypothesis is always the summary of some special experience universalized. That does not mean that the past is worthless. Politics, as Seeley said, are vulgar unless they are liberalized by history; and a State which failed to see itself as a mosaic of ancestral institutions would build its novelties upon foundations of sand. Suspicion of collective effort in the eighteenth century ought not to mean suspicion in the twentieth; to think in such fashion is to fall into the error for which Lassalle so finely criticized Hegel. It is as though one were to confound the accidental phases of the history of property with the philosophic basis of property itself. From such an error it is the task of history above all to free us. For it records the ideals and doubts of earlier ages as a perennial challenge to the coming time.

The rightness of this attitude admits of proof in terms of the double tradition to which Adam Smith gave birth. On the one hand he is the founder of the classic political economy. With Ricardo, the elder Mill, and Nassau Senior, the main preoccupation is the production of wealth without regard to its moral environment; and the State for them is merely an engine to protect the atmosphere in which business men achieve their labours. There is nothing in them of that fine despair which made Stuart Mill welcome socialism itself rather than allow the continuance of the new capitalist system. Herein the State is purged of moral purpose; and the utilitarian method achieves the greatest happiness by insisting that the technique of production must dominate all other circumstances. Until the Reform Act of 1867, the orthodox economists remained unchallenged. The use of the franchise was only beginning to be understood. The 'new model' of trade-unionism had not yet been tested in the political field. But it was discovered impossible to act any longer upon the assumptions of the abstract economic man. The infallible sense of his own interest was discovered to be without basis in the facts for the simple reason that the instruments of his perception obviously required training if they were to be applied to a complex world. Individualism, in the old, utilitarian sense, passed away because it failed to build a State wherein a channel of expression might be found for the creative energies of humble men.

It is only within recent decades that we have begun to understand the inner significance of the protest against this economic liberalism. Adam Smith had declared the source of value to lie in labour; and, at the moment of its deepest agony, there were men willing to point the moral of his tale. That it represented an incautious analysis was, for them, unimportant beside the fact that it opened once more a path whereby economics could be reclaimed for moral science. For if labour was the source of value, as Bray and Thompson pointed out, it seemed as though degradation was the sole payment for its services. They did not ask whether

the organization they envisaged was economically profitable, but whether it was ethically right. No one can
read the history of these years and fail to understand
their uncompromising denial of its rightness. Their
negation fell upon unheeding ears; but twenty years
later, the tradition for which they stood came into
Marx's hands and was fashioned by him into an interpretation of history. With all its faults of statement and
of emphasis, the doctrine of the English socialists has
been, in later hands, the most fruitful hypothesis of
modern politics. It was a deliberate effort, upon the
basis of Adam Smith's ideas, to create a commonwealth
in the interests of the masses. Wealth, in its view, was
less the mere production of goods than the accumulated
happiness of humble men. The impulses it praised and
sought through State action to express were, indeed,
different from those upon which Smith laid emphasis;
and he would doubtless have stood aghast at the way
in which his thought was turned to ends of which he
did not dream. Yet he can hardly have desired a greater
glory. He thus made possible not only knowledge of a
State untrammelled in its economic life by moral considerations; but also the road to those categories wherein
the old conception of co-operative effort might find a
new expression. Those who trod in his footsteps may
have repudiated the ideal for which he stood, but they
made possible a larger hope in which he would have
been proud and glad to share.

# BIBLIOGRAPHY

*This bibliography makes no pretence to completeness. It attempts only to enumerate the more obvious sources that an interested reader would care to examine.*

## GENERAL

LESLIE STEPHEN. *History of English Thought in the Eighteenth Century.* 1876. Vol. II, Chapters IX and X.

W. E. H. LECKY. *History of England in the Eighteenth Century.*

A. L. SMITH. *Political Philosophy in England in the Seventeenth and Eighteenth Centuries* in the *Cambridge Modern History.* Vol. VI, Chapter XXIII.

J. BONAR. *Philosophy and Political Economy.* Chapters V–IX.

F. W. MAITLAND. *An Historical Sketch of Liberty and Equality* in *Collected Papers.* Vol. I.

## Chapter II

JOHN LOCKE. *Works* (Eleventh Edition), 10 volumes. London, 1812.

H. R. FOX-BOURNE. *Life of John Locke.* London, 1876.

T. H. GREEN. *The Principles of Political Obligation* in *Collected Works.* Vol. II. London, 1908.

PETER, LORD KING. *The Life and Letters of John Locke.* London, 1858.

SIR F. POLLOCK. *Locke's Theory of the State* in *Proc. Brit. Acad.* Vol. I. London, 1904.

S. P. LAMPRECHT. *The Moral and Political Philosophy of Locke*. New York, 1918.

A. A. SEATON. *The Theory of Toleration under the Later Stuarts*. Cambridge, 1911.

J. N. FIGGIS. *The Divine Right of Kings*. Cambridge, 1914.

## Chapter III

JEREMY COLLIER. *The History of Passive Obedience*. London, 1689.

WILLIAM SHERLOCK. *The Case of Resistance*. London, 1684.

CHARLES LESLIE. *The Case of the Regale* (Collected Works). Vol. III, p. 291.
  *The Rehearsal.*
  *The New Association.*
  *Cassandra.*
  *The Finishing Stroke.*
  *Obedience to Civil Government Clearly Stated.*
  *The Best Answer.*
  *The Best of All.*

SAMUEL GRASCOM. *A Brief Answer.*

E. STILLINGFLEET. *A Vindication of their Majesties Authoritie.*

B. SHOWER. *A Letter to a Convocation Man.*

W. WAKE. *The Authority of Christian Princes.*
  *The State of the Church* (1703).

FRANCIS ATTERBURY. *Rights, Powers and Privileges of an English Convocation* (1701).

BENJAMIN HOADLY. *Origins of Civil Government* (1710).
  *Preservative Against Nonjurors* (1716).
  *Works.* 3 vols. London (1773).

WILLIAM LAW. *A Defence of Church Principles* (ed. Gore). Edinburgh, 1904.

W. WARBURTON. *Alliance between Church and State* (1736).

J. H. OVERTON. *The Nonjurors*. New York, 1903.

T. LATHBURY. *History of Convocation*. London, 1842.

## Chapter IV

BERKELEY. *Essay Towards Preventing the Ruin of Great Britain* (1721).

H. ST. JOHN (Viscount Bolingbroke). *Works.* 5 vols. London, 1754.

LORD EGMONT. *Faction detected by the Evidence of Facts* (1742).

DAVID HUME. *Inquiry Concerning the Principles of Morals* (1752).
  *Essays* (1742–1752) ed. Green & Grose. London, 1876.

W. SICHEL. *Life of Bolingbroke.* 2 vols. 1900–4.

J. CHURTON COLLINS. *Bolingbroke and Voltaire in England.*

J. HILL BURTON. *Life of Hume.*

## Chapter V

MONTESQUIEU. *L'Esprit des Lois* (1748).

J. J. ROUSSEAU. *Du Contrat Social* (1762). See ed. by Vaughan, 1918.

JOHN BROWN. *Estimate of the Manners and Principles of the Times* (1757).

ADAM FERGUSON. *Essay on the History of Civil Society* (1767).

WILLIAM BLACKSTONE. *Commentaries* (1765–9).

JEREMY BENTHAM. *A Fragment on Government* (1776). Ed. F. C. Montague, 1891.

J. DE LOLME. *The Constitution of England* (1775).

ROBERT WALLACE. *Various Prospects* (1761).

JOSEPH PRIESTLEY. *Essay on the First Principles of Government* (1768).

RICHARD PRICE. *Observations on Civil Liberty* (1776).
  *Additional Observations* (1777).

WILLIAM OGILVIE. *The Right of Property in Land* (1781). Ed. Macdonald, 1891.

JOSIAH TUCKER. *Treatise on Civil Government* (1781).
SAMUEL JOHNSON. *Taxation No Tyranny* (1775).
M. BEER. *History of British Socialism* (1919).
JAMES BOSWELL. *Life of Samuel Johnson* (1791).
ROLAND THOMAS. *Life of Richard Price* (1924).


## Chapter VI

EDMUND BURKE. *Collected Works.* London, 1808.
JOHN MORLEY. *Edmund Burke* (1867).
    *Life of Burke* (1887).
J. MACCUNN. *The Political Philosophy of Burke* (1908).
JUNIUS. *Letters* (1769–72). London, 1812.
THOMAS PAINE. *The Rights of Man* (1791–2).
JAMES MACKINTOSH. *Vindiciae Gallicae* (1791).
RICHARD LENNOX. *Edmund Burke.* Berlin, 1923.


## Chapter VII

CHARLES DAVENANT. *Works.* London, 1771.
SIR DUDLEY NORTH. *A Discourse upon Trade* (1691).
ADAM SMITH. *Theory of Moral Sentiments* (1759).
    *The Wealth of Nations* (1776).
    *Lectures on Justice and Police.* (Ed. Cannan, 1896.)
W. R. SCOTT. *Life of Francis Hutcheson* (1900).
JOHN RAE. *Life of Adam Smith* (1895).
W. BAGEHOT. *Adam Smith as a Person* in *Coll. Works.*
    Vol. VII.
F. W. HIRST. *Adam Smith* (1904).
W. HASBACH. *Untersüchungen über Adam Smith* (1891).
J. BONAR. *A Catalogue of Adam Smith's Library* (1894).
T. CLIFFE LESLIE. *Adam Smith* in *Essays in Moral and
    Political Philosophy* (1879).
E. TROELTSCH. *Die Sociallehren der Christlichen Kirchen*
    (1912).
R. H. TAWNEY. *Religion and Capitalism* (1926).

# INDEX

PRINTED IN GREAT BRITAIN BY THE RIVERSIDE PRESS, EDINBURGH